The International Equity Commitment

The Institute of Chartered Financial Analysts is a subsidiary of the Association for Investment Management and Research.

ISBN 0-943205-44-1

Printed in the United States of America

August 1998

Editorial Staff
Roger Mitchell
Editor

Fiona D. Russell Cowen
Assistant Editor

Jaynee M. Dudley
Production Manager

Christine P. Martin
Production Coordinator

Lois A. Carrier and Diane B. Hamshar
Composition

Mission

The Research Foundation's mission is to identify, fund, and publish research that is relevant to the AIMR Global Body of Knowledge and useful for AIMR member investment practitioners and investors.

Biography of the Author

Stephen A. Gorman, CFA, is vice president and senior quantitative analyst in the global asset allocation group at Putnam Investments, where he specializes in strategic asset allocation, portfolio construction, and tactical country model development. Previously, he has held positions at AT&T; Pell Rudman, Boston Harbor Trust Company; Applied Economics, and *Investment Dealers' Digest*. Mr. Gorman is the author of several articles on asset allocation. He holds a B.A. from the College of the Holy Cross and an M.B.A. from the Amos Tuck School at Dartmouth College.

Contents

Foreword   viii

Acknowledgments   x

Chapter 1.   Introduction.   1

Chapter 2.   The International Equity Commitment   5

Chapter 3.   Benchmarking and Historical Perspective   39

Chapter 4.   Key Fundamentals: Currency,
             Correlations, and Costs   57

Chapter 5.   Conclusion.   96

Appendix   97

References   103

Selected Publications   110

Foreword

A short while back, I had the opportunity to travel to Asia to interview portfolio managers about that region's financial crisis. The downturn was already more than a year old at the time of my trip, and like many finance professionals from outside that part of the world, I assumed that the worst had nearly passed and that the conditions would soon return to normal. According to the money managers I spoke with, however, nothing could have been further from truth. Indeed, to a person, these market specialists predicted that the region would only get back to business as usual after some fundamental and potentially painful economic reforms at both the government and corporate levels. All told, the trip was quite enlightening—and more than a little shocking—for someone who had always imagined himself reasonably well-versed in the ways of global capital markets.

I suspect that my experience was not unique, particularly for those of us who exist in the relative geographical isolation of the United States. Nevertheless, it does raise an interesting question: Why are most investors not better equipped to evaluate economic conditions and investment opportunities beyond their own borders? The answer certainly cannot be that we misunderstand the potential benefits. Since the pioneering work of Harry Markowitz in the 1950s, investment professionals have known how to reduce and control portfolio risk by diversifying investments into different types of securities and asset classes. Further, H. G. Grubel and Bruno Solnik extended these basic findings over the next two decades to demonstrate the additional advantages of diversifying portfolios with the inclusion of international securities. Given how long these theoretical prescriptions have been available, any failure to implement them can only be attributed to either investor ignorance—an unlikely event in markets generally regarded as efficient—or practical difficulties that make international investing difficult and cost ineffective.

In this monograph, Stephen Gorman attempts to reconcile the theoretical benefits with the practical realities of making foreign equity investments. Early on, he justifies the need for a project of this nature with a truly remarkable statistic: As recently as 1996, only 1 out of every 10 dollars invested by U.S.-based pension funds went into foreign assets, an amount that would have to increase by about 60 percent to match the international commitment of these funds' counterparts in the rest of the developed world. This underallocation to global investments also comes at a time when most pension funds have had trouble beating their performance benchmarks. Not surprisingly, such pressure on the bottom line has caused many managers and plan sponsors to reevaluate their investment policies in order to purge any explicit or

©The Research Foundation of the ICFA

unintentional provincialism. The question is, in the face of myriad institutional, cultural, and informational barriers, how should this new resolve be set in motion?

Gorman lays out the blueprint for an intelligent approach to foreign equity investing in chapter two, which is really the heart of the monograph, and argues that such a commitment demands a combination of theoretical, strategic, and tactical viewpoints. The strategic view, which he defines as the process of modifying the recommendations of international portfolio and capital asset pricing theory for practical considerations, commands the most attention. For instance, although theory suggests a long-run, buy-and-hold position in a well-diversified portfolio containing a roughly two-thirds allocation to non-U.S. stocks, the shorter-term focus of most asset managers might dictate otherwise. How and what investors should do in these situations is the author's primary concern. In particular, Gorman does an excellent job of advising readers of the problems that can (and do) arise when forecasting return and risk parameters over shorter time horizons.

The remaining chapters of the monograph address a wide array of additional issues, such as the composition of international equity indexes, currency exposure, correlation forecasting, foreign fiscal and monetary policy, and transaction costs. Of course, each of these topics can at times be a crucial consideration in the proper maintenance of a global investment program, and this material adds considerable depth to the policy-oriented discussions that start the monograph and creates a complete and well-balanced treatment.

In the past year, the Research Foundation of the Institute of Chartered Financial Analysts has published *Emerging Stock Markets: Risk, Return, and Performance* by Christopher Barry, John Peavy, and Mauricio Rodriquez and *Country Risk in Global Financial Management* by Claude Erb, Campbell Harvey, and Tadas Viskanta, two works that have given investors a great deal of practical guidance about the costs and benefits of overseas investment. With the publication of *The International Equity Commitment*, the Research Foundation extends its own commitment to providing readers with the most cogent and topical material possible on this important topic. Gorman has done a first-rate job of synthesizing many of the arguments and counterarguments that define the debate, and the resulting work is a valuable user's guide for both experienced practitioners and those considering these issues for the first time. We are quite pleased to bring it to your attention.

Keith C. Brown, CFA
Research Director
The Research Foundation of the
Institute of Chartered Financial Analysts

Acknowledgments

I am grateful for the insights, perspective, and editorial comments provided by the following senior investment professionals at Putnam Investments: Tim Ferguson, Bill Landes, Jeff Knight, Bill Zieff, Erik Knutzen, Debbie Kuenstner, Tom Haslett, and Robert Swift. I would also like to thank the numerous specialists who provided data at FactSet; Goldman, Sachs & Company; Salomon Brothers Inc; Lehman Brothers; Merrill Lynch & Company; Morgan Stanley; and the International Finance Corporation. Finally, I appreciate the support of the Research Foundation of the Institute of Chartered Financial Analysts and AIMR.

©The Research Foundation of the ICFA

1. Introduction

Three decades have passed since Grubel (1968) published a seminal article touting the benefits of international diversification. Extending the work of Markowitz (1959) and Tobin (1958), Grubel used return data from 11 non-U.S. stock markets to demonstrate that U.S. investors could have increased their portfolio returns at reduced levels of return volatility by purchasing international equities during the period from 1959 to 1966. In the years following the publication of this article, a legion of practitioners and academics built upon Grubel's work and ushered in the era of globally conscious U.S. investment management.

Although some U.S. plan sponsors incorporated significant international equity positions into their portfolios during the 1970s and 1980s, many have been slow to embrace fully international diversification. As Table 1.1 indicates, almost 90 percent of U.S. assets are still invested domestically, which exceeds the domestic holdings in most countries with developed pension systems. U.S. institutions pension plans would need to increase their current 1996 aggregate international commitment by roughly $300 billion, or 60 percent, to match the commitment maintained by their counterparts in other developed markets. With respect to the equity portfolio, the cross-border commitment of the typical U.S. pension plan is less than half that of the typical non-U.S. pension plan.[1]

Such trepidation by U.S. plan sponsors with respect to international equity exposure is unlikely to disappear anytime soon. In the 1990s, as a result of the combination of the "post-bubble" Japanese equity market and the sizzling U.S. equity market, the Morgan Stanley Capital International (MSCI) EAFE (Europe/Australasia/Far East) Index has underperformed the MSCI U.S. Index significantly, as shown in Table 1.2. In addition to concerns regarding rising intermarket return correlations, disruptive exchange rate volatility, and insurmountable transaction costs, this underperformance has led many plan sponsors to reevaluate their commitment to international equity. One alternative devised by plan sponsors is to refine the strategic mandate for non-U.S.

---

[1]According to the Investment Company Institute (ICI), as of December 1996, the average individual investor in the U.S. holds a position similar to U.S. pension plans. Of the $2,637 billion in reported mutual fund holdings in the United States, only $321 billion, or 12 percent, is invested abroad (principally in stocks). See the ICI report *Trends in Mutual Fund Activity* (January 1997).

Table 1.1   Global Pension Assets, December 1996

Country	Total Assets (US$ billions)	Foreign Assets as Share of Total Assets [a]	Foreign Equity as Share of Total Equity
United States	$4,352	11%	16%
Japan	1,142	15	35
United Kingdom	1,058	26	29
Netherlands	350	21	58
Canada	306	18	27
Switzerland	257	12	46
Germany	131	5	22
Italy	80	1	—
France	74	7	—
Other developed markets	418	13	34
Total (excluding U.S.)	$3,816	17%	35%

[a]Majority of cross-border assets are in stocks.

Sources: Watson Wyatt Worldwide and InterSec Research Corporation.

investments to include only value, small-capitalization, or emerging market stocks. Another idea is to give global managers the tactical latitude to invest abroad but to measure them against a U.S. equity benchmark. Before concluding that recent history represents the dawn of a new relative-performance era, however, investors should note that the recent experience depicted in Table 1.2 is not the first extended period of poor relative international performance and that such return differentials have a history of reverting to the mean, as shown in Figure 1.1.

With this ongoing debate in mind, the purpose of this monograph is to justify a significant strategic allocation to international equity markets, both developed and emerging, and to raise the general level of understanding of the issues surrounding international diversification—specifically, benchmarks, currency, correlations, and costs.

Determining the Proper Allocation

No method of promoting international diversification has been used (and

Table 1.2.   MSCI EAFE Index Underperformance Relative to the MSCI U.S. Index, January 1990–December 1996
(unhedged returns)

	United States	EAFE	Japan	EAFE ex Japan
Average return	15.7%	5.4%	−1.2%	12.7%
Standard deviation	13.3	18.6	27.0	15.6

Source: MSCI.

Figure 1.1. International Equity Premium Disaggregation, December 1970–December 1996

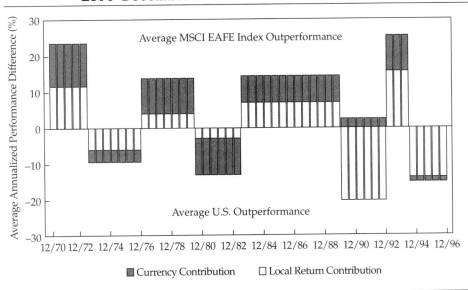

Sources: Based on data from MSCI and Standard and Poor's.

misused) more regularly than the efficient frontier analysis shown in Figure 1.2.[2] This incarnation illustrates the benefits that were available to an unhedged U.S. investor over the past 27 years (and will be available in the future, assuming that the past is prologue—a big assumption). By investing three-quarters of the equity portfolio abroad, the optimally diversified U.S. investor outpaced the U.S. equity market by 110 basis points a year with no increase in return volatility.

The "optimal" international equity allocation in Figure 1.2 is several times greater than the 16 percent held by the average U.S. pension plan. Clearly, plan sponsors are justified in tempering any inference drawn from such a simple historical analysis. Unfortunately, overemphasizing legitimate concerns or relying on common misconceptions regarding international investing often obscures the simple message of Figure 1.2. The long-term evidence is insufficient to conclude that international equity has failed to deliver attractive diversification benefits. Put another way, on the basis of past data, investors

---

[2]Technically, Figure 1.1 depicts the minimum-variance frontier. The efficient frontier extends from the minimum-variance portfolio to the maximum-return portfolio, so portfolios containing more than 62 percent U.S. equity are inefficient. Also, this sample illustration obviously overstates the attractiveness of international developed market equity because of the omission of the many other asset classes typically included in pension portfolios.

Figure 1.2. Historical Efficient Frontier: MSCI U.S. Index and MSCI EAFE Index, January 1970–December 1996

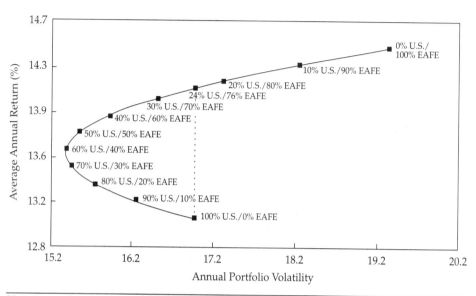

Note: Intervals on return scale may appear irregular because of rounding.
Source: Based on data from MSCI.

cannot reject the null hypothesis of investment theory that global diversification makes sense. This point is developed extensively in this monograph, which makes the challenge not to justify international equity exposure but to determine the proper amount.

In short, developing an appropriate policy mix is the most important challenge a plan sponsor faces.[3] Determining the proper international equity allocation is a major part of meeting this challenge, so plan sponsors must carefully consider the broad array of relevant issues, whether as mundane as benchmark methodology or as academic as asset-pricing theory. As plan sponsors are well aware, critically evaluating the output of a portfolio-construction process (quantitative or otherwise) while satisfying the ERISA (Employee Retirement Income Security Act of 1974) requirements of diligence, prudence, and care is difficult, especially without a thorough grounding in such matters. This monograph meets the need for information by providing a fresh and practical perspective on the key issues of international equity.

---

[3]Brinson, Hood, and Beebower (1986) and Brinson, Singer, and Beebower (1991). For a different perspective on the same data, see Jahnke (1997).

©The Research Foundation of the ICFA

2. The International Equity Commitment

The commitment to international equity requires the synthesis of equilibrium, strategic, and tactical views. *Equilibrium views* reflect the theoretical underpinnings of a long-term international equity position. *Strategic views* adjust the equilibrium views to reflect the practical shortcomings of theory. *Tactical views* supplement the strategic views to ensure that a portfolio remains on course to meet its investment objectives. That is, generating strategic views is a process fraught with difficulties and potentially large forecast errors, and even prescient strategic views do not insulate a portfolio against undesirable outcomes from accurately specified return distributions. Tactical asset allocation (TAA) mitigates the effects of such problems by bringing additional information to the investment management process.

Each set of views influences the fundamental assumptions that determine portfolio structure—expected returns, volatilities, and correlations. To understand how equilibrium, strategic, and tactical views might flow together in the portfolio construction process, consider the following example using correlations: To construct equilibrium views, an investment manager uses correlations based on long-term historical data, perhaps weighted to de-emphasize less applicable historical periods. Once the equilibrium views are established, the manager makes strategic adjustments based, for example, on five-year correlations conditioned on global economic growth expectations. Finally, the manager modifies the strategic views on the basis of tactical views, including quarterly correlations forecasts generated by a GARCH (generalized autoregressive conditional heteroscedasticity) model. As this example makes clear, and as this chapter demonstrates in detail, each of the three areas has implications for the policy mix.

The Equilibrium Case for International Equity

Finance theory indicates that investors in all countries should hold the same collection of risky assets—the partially hedged global market portfolio (GMP). The GMP is composed of all the tradable assets in the world, each of which may be hedged in a unique way against exchange rate risk.[1] A rough estimate of the GMP's composition is shown in Table 2.1.

---

[1] See Solnik (1974a) and Odier and Solnik (1993) for a derivation of this theory.

Table 2.1.   Global Capitalization and Economic Significance, December 1996

(US$ billions)

Country/Region	Bonds		Stocks		Capitalization		GNP	
United States	$9,801	42%	$7,836	40%	$17,637	42%	$7,100	26%
Japan	4,140	18	3,071	16	7,211	17	4,964	18
Germany	2,717	12	648	3	3,365	8	2,252	8
United Kingdom	685	3	1,740	9	2,425	6	1,095	4
France	1,051	5	601	3	1,651	4	1,451	5
G–5 countries	$18,394	80%	$13,896	72%	$32,290	76%	$16,862	61%
Italy	1,286	6	253	1	1,538	4	1,088	4
Canada	485	2	464	2	949	2	574	2
Netherlands	388	2	393	2	781	2	371	1
Switzerland	242	1	407	2	649	2	286	1
G–9 countries	$20,795	90%	$15,412	79%	$36,207	85%	$19,181	69%
Other developed countries	1,764	8	1,749	9	3,513	8	3,328	12
Emerging countries	535	2	2,228	11	2,763	7	5,179	19
Global total	$23,094	100%	$19,389	100%	$42,483	100%	$27,687	100%
G–9 ex United States	10,994	83	7,576	66	18,571	75	12,081	59
All other	2,299	17	3,977	34	6,276	25	8,507	41
Non-U.S. total	$13,294	100%	$11,553	100%	$24,846	100%	$20,587	100%

Note: Columns may not add to totals because of rounding. Data are for financial assets only; the "true" GMP would include all tradable assets.

Sources: Based on data from the IFC, Merrill Lynch & Company, Salomon Smith Barney, and Morgan Stanley Capital International.

The GMP, as shown in Figure 2.1, establishes the point at which the capital market line is tangent to the set of all possible risky portfolios (i.e., the point of maximum reward to variability) and is, therefore, the *only* risky portfolio investors should own (barring restrictions). Investors take positions in the GMP commensurate with their risk tolerance. Conservative investors hold portions of their wealth in risk-free U.S. Treasury bills and invest the remainder in the GMP, thereby attaining points on the capital market line to the left of the global market portfolio. Conversely, aggressive investors, by borrowing funds and taking leveraged positions in the GMP, achieve positions on the capital market line to the right of the global market portfolio.

The GMP carries such distinction because the international capital asset pricing model (ICAPM) presupposes that, on average and over time, investors are compensated only for assuming systematic or market risk, not for

Figure 2.1. The International Capital Asset Pricing Model

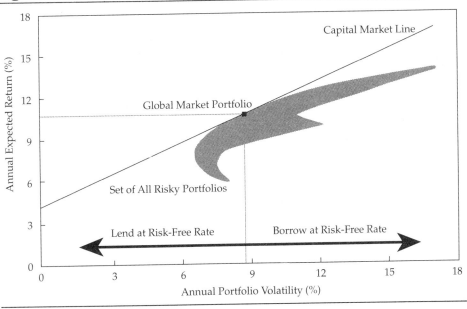

accepting risks that can be diversified away by purchasing other asset classes. The algebraic expression of the ICAPM is as follows:

$$E\left[\text{Return}_{Portfolio}\right] = \text{Return}_{RF} + \sum_{i=1}^{n} \beta_{Asset\ i, GMP}(\text{Risk premium}_{GMP})w_i$$

$$+ \sum_{i=1}^{n}\sum_{j=1}^{m} \gamma_{Asset\ i, Currency\ j}(\text{Risk premium}_{Currency\ j})w_i w_j,$$

where

$E[\text{Return}_{Portfolio}]$	= expected portfolio return
Return_{RF}	= risk-free return
β	= the standardized return covariance of the ith asset with the global market portfolio (given n assets)
γ	= the standardized return covariance of the ith asset with the jth currency (given m exchange rates)
w	= the weight in the ith asset or the jth currency

The transition from equation to graph, as shown in Figure 2.1, is basic (setting aside currencies). Because all the portfolios on the capital market line have only systematic risk and thus are perfectly correlated, or (with ρ as correlation and σ as covariance)

$$\rho_{Portfolio, \, GMP} = \frac{\sigma_{Portfolio, \, GMP}}{\sigma_{Portfolio}\sigma_{GMP}} = 1,$$

$\beta_{Portfolio, \, GMP}$ can be expressed as

$$\frac{\sigma_{Portfolio}}{\sigma_{GMP}},$$

which yields the equation of the capital market line:

$$R_{Portfolio} = R_{RF} + \frac{R_{GMP} - R_{RF}}{\sigma_{GMP}} \sigma_{Portfolio}.$$

With respect to global equity, use of the ICAPM is straightforward and, given the data in Table 2.1, suggests the following allocation:

U.S. equity	40%
International developed market equity	49
Emerging market equity	11

On the currency side, however, the time-varying nature of the risk premium in the ICAPM creates difficulty in specifying the appropriate country-level hedge ratios. A tempting way to deal with this problem in an equilibrium context is to use purchasing power parity and the zero hedge ratio implied by PPP. Although PPP ultimately may prove to be a reasonable basis for establishing equilibrium currency views, real exchange rates do fluctuate and protracted periods of disequilibrium have been common, so PPP is no panacea. As a result (and for the reasons discussed in Chapter 4), a 50 percent equilibrium hedge ratio should be applied in the developed non-U.S. markets and a zero hedge ratio must be accepted in the emerging markets because of the obstacles to hedging in emerging currency markets.[2]

The Strategic Case for International Equity

As the investment analogue to the adage about not putting all your eggs in the same basket, the ICAPM represents a useful starting point in constructing a strategic portfolio[3] and provides an intuitively appealing theoretical precedent for acknowledging the size of international markets during this process. As

---

[2]The universal hedge ratio of Black (1989), because of its simplifying assumptions (e.g., homogeneous investor risk tolerance), represents a practical alternative to the ICAPM currency exposure problem. Given the discrepancies between these assumptions and reality, however, the universal hedge ratio does not appear any more appropriate than the 50 percent ratio assumed here.

[3]Note that the terms strategic portfolio, policy portfolio, benchmark portfolio, neutral portfolio, and normal portfolio are used interchangeably throughout this monograph.

Table 2.1 indicates, approximately 60 percent of global financial assets and 75 percent of global gross national product (GNP) are located outside the United States. (The eight major non-U.S. developed markets account for 75 percent and 60 percent, respectively, of these totals.) Theory has provided the null hypothesis favoring a significant international equity allocation, so the burden of proof must rest with arguments to reduce or change the complexion of that diversification.

As with any theoretical construct, investment managers must reckon with the ICAPM's practical limitations. The ICAPM is not a panacea for the many portfolio construction problems faced by plan sponsors. Inconsistencies between reality and the assumptions underlying the ICAPM warrant regular departures from the theoretical, or neutral, allocations. The asset class weights in the GMP may prove suboptimal because the global marketplace is either not completely efficient or not completely integrated. Inefficiencies and country-level influences on security returns result in partially segmented markets.[4] Furthermore, the benchmarked, investable world differs from the capitalization weights presented in Table 2.1. Based on the Morgan Stanley Capital International (MSCI) World Index (excluding Malaysia) and the International Finance Corporation (IFC) Investable Composite Index, the equilibrium equity allocations would change as follows:[5]

	Capitalization	Benchmarked
U.S. equity	40%	41%
International developed market equity	49	53
Emerging market equity	11	6

In addition, the optimality of equilibrium allocations may be undone by factors such as differences in return and volatility forecasts among investment professionals (the ICAPM assumes homogeneous expectations), the existence of taxes and transaction costs (the ICAPM assumes none), differences in investment horizon (the ICAPM assumes a single, universal time frame), leverage restrictions (the ICAPM assumes unlimited borrowing and lending in any currency), and multiple sources of systematic risk (the ICAPM assumes that β_{GMP} is the only one). Finally, the ICAPM presupposes that all investors rely on mean–variance analysis and that they hold a well-defined global market portfolio. In actuality, many approaches to portfolio construction exist, biases toward domestic equity holdings are widespread, and the market portfolio is a somewhat nebulous concept.

---

[4]Chapter 3 provides a more detailed analysis of such factors.

[5]Malaysia is included in both the MSCI EAFE and IFC Investable indexes. Because the World Bank classifies Malaysia as a middle-income economy, it is included among the emerging, not the developed markets, in this monograph. Also, Canada is included in the MSCI World Index but not in the EAFE Index.

Table 2.2. U.S. and International Developed Market Equity, January 1978–December 1996

Measure	United States	50 Percent Hedged International Developed Markets	
		Representation I	Representation II
Average return	16.8%	16.0%	17.6%
Standard deviation	16.8%	17.2%	16.2%
Correlation with United States	—	0.50	0.60

Source: MSCI.

Despite its warts, the ICAPM should anchor the strategic portfolio construction process. Although markets oscillate around their neutral levels (at times deviating considerably and for extended periods of time from those levels), because investors eventually force markets back toward equilibrium—that is, back toward the ICAPM—the ICAPM is the best candidate available to provide equilibrium asset allocation perspective and, therefore, must be considered in the portfolio construction process.

The Strategic Portfolio Problem. What the ICAPM does not do is obviate the need to perform strategic analyses. Passively holding the global market portfolio may turn out to be optimal in the very long run but almost certainly not over the three- to five-year strategic planning horizon of many plan sponsors. Although a longer horizon makes sense, given the liability structure of most pension plans, the reality of strategic asset allocation is that the adequacy of a policy mix is judged over a relatively short time period. In the interest of diligence, most plan sponsors revisit the policy mix at least on an annual basis as new information becomes available and is incorporated into forecasts.

Over a time period of three to five years, as a consequence of the aforementioned theoretical shortcomings and sampling error from equilibrium return distributions, many country combinations have been and will be more efficient than the global market portfolio. The challenge faced by investment managers and plan sponsors, given a finite planning and performance evaluation period, is to make prudent *ex ante* departures from the ICAPM allocations in favor of more efficient portfolios.

Many investors attempt to meet this challenge by using historical return series to derive inputs to a mean–variance optimizer that generates a strategic asset mix. Because optimization results are sensitive to input specification, however, blind reliance on historical data is perilous. This observation is most true for expected-return inputs. Mean–variance optimization results are about 10 times more sensitive to expected-return specifications than to standard deviation assumptions, which are roughly twice as important as correlation inputs.[6]

Consider the equity returns over the past two decades, as shown in Table 2.2. Representation I of international equity performance is simply the conventional MSCI EAFE (Europe/Australasia/Far East) Index. Representation II is the MSCI World Index, excluding the United States and Malaysia, with historical country weights fixed at the levels in effect in December 1996. This approach eliminates the impact of the Japanese bubble on historical EAFE returns because the prospect of Japan's index weighting ever again being twice its current level is unlikely.

Given Representation I, an optimizer views U.S. equity as the dominant asset class and recommends no allocation to international equity. If Representation II is used, the exact opposite is true—no allocation to U.S. equity. Under either set of assumptions, the rolling three-year optimizations in Table 2.3 reveal that partially hedged international equity was the dominant asset class throughout the 1980s and that U.S. equity has been dominant in the 1990s. As a result, the average allocation of these three-year portfolios is approximately 50 percent U.S. and 50 percent non-U.S. equity.

Depending on whether Representation I or II is used, this average portfolio offered a 40 basis point (bp) increase (II) or decrease (I) in mean return relative to a U.S. equity portfolio, but it provided a 200 bp reduction in volatility under either representation. Similar results are obtained if the average international equity return is adjusted up (I) or down (II) by only 80 bps, as demonstrated by "Optimization Results for Entire Period" in Table 2.3. Such an adjustment is trivial in the context of equity return variance. In fact, not only is the 80 bp return difference statistically insignificant but to conclude otherwise would require monthly return series dating back to the collapse of the Persian Empire 1,400 years ago for Representation II and to the zenith of the Roman Empire 1,800 years ago for Representation I.[7]

Granted that any historical analysis suffers to some extent from sample dependence, these results can be interpreted conservatively as inconclusive on the international equity issue or, more reasonably, as supportive of a significant strategic international equity allocation. Either way, no compelling historical evidence supports a reduction in the small existing international stake of the typical pension plan.

---

[6]See Chopra and Ziemba (1993).

[7]$n_{Months} = [2.96]^2 \sigma^2_{Monthly\ return\ differences} / \mu^2_{Monthly\ return\ difference}$, assuming serially independent and homoscedastic return distributions, where n is the number of months, σ^2 is variance, and m is the mean.

Table 2.3. Rolling Three-Year Historical Optimizations, January 1978–December 1996

Three Years Ended	Representation I (percent)	Representation II (percent)
Optimal portfolio (U.S./international)		
12/80	0/100	0/100
12/81	0/100	0/100
12/82	100/0	100/0
12/83	0/100	0/100
12/84	0/100	0/100
12/85	0/100	0/100
12/86	22/78	8/92
12/87	0/100	0/100
12/88	7/93	0/100
12/89	0/100	0/100
12/90	100/0	100/0
12/91	100/0	100/0
12/92	100/0	100/0
12/93	100/0	100/0
12/94	82/18	82/18
12/95	100/0	73/27
12/96	100/0	100/0
Average of rolling three-year optimizations		
Portfolio	48/52	45/55
Expected return	16.4%	17.2%
Volatility	14.7%	14.7%
	Optimization Results for Entire Period	
Optimal portfolio given historical expected returns		
Portfolio	100/0	0/100
Expected return	16.8%	17.6%
Volatility	16.8%	16.2%
Optimal portfolio given equal expected returns		
Portfolio	53/47	46/54
Expected return	16.8%	16.8%
Volatility	14.7%	14.7%

Note: Optimal portfolio anchored to the volatility of a U.S. equity portfolio; annualized summary statistics.

■ *Three uncertainties.* The forward-looking strategic asset allocation problem results from three uncertainties. First, the past is not prologue. Investment managers must make prospective statements about returns, and the answers do not fall out of historical return series or an equilibrium model (i.e., the ICAPM). Such an obvious point merits mention because the rearview mirror can exert a powerful influence on investment managers and plan sponsors. In other words, to regret not having a larger strategic allocation to the U.S. equity market during the past few years is one thing, but to extrapolate recent U.S. outperformance into the future and thus justify a smaller strategic international equity position is quite another.

Another uncertainty is that, although the *sum* of the historical evidence is insufficient to refute the null hypothesis favoring a significant international equity allocation, return differences over a single strategic planning period can be enormous. Figure 2.2 illustrates potential five-year performance differences between the United States and the partially hedged international developed markets, assuming equal means and variances and a correlation of 0.6. A return disparity of 1,000 bp a year for five years is not even a two-standard-deviation event, and international underperformance over the five years ending December 1996 is barely a one-standard-deviation event. (For those who find this observation surprising, a few historical five-year performance differentials are plotted in Figure 2.2 to illustrate how actual experience compares with this potential distribution.) Although a TAA program is an important tool for mitigating the impact of such potentially gaping return disparities, uncertainty remains because prudent, risk-minded policy setting is incapable of completely capturing such extreme performance differentials.

The third uncertainty is accuracy of forecasts. Unfortunately, the investment management community is incapable of countering return variability with accurate three- to five-year return projections. In other words, investment managers and plan sponsors are accountable *ex post* for large strategic performance differentials but can do precious little about them *ex ante*. This problem is compounded by two characteristics of the output of a typical portfolio optimizer:

- Results magnify forecast errors. For example, an overstated return forecast inflates expected portfolio performance, partly because of the error itself and partly because the error is spread across a greater allocation to that asset than would otherwise be the case. Magnification of errors is a particular problem in the case of equity portfolio optimization because large errors inevitably accompany equity return forecasts.

Figure 2.2. Potential Return Differentials between Partially Hedged International Developed and U.S. Equity Markets over Five-Year Periods, 1978–96

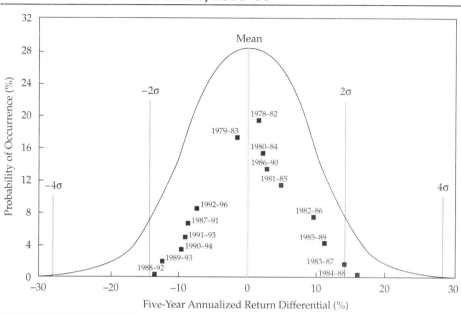

Notes: Histogram assumes identical means with 16.8 percent standard deviation and 0.6 correlation.

- Results can be extremely sensitive to small differences in return forecasts, and allocations to asset classes in the same volatility region (i.e., asset classes that have comparable return variance) are particularly vulnerable. Such sensitivity also is a major issue in equity portfolio optimization because the similar volatility of U.S. and partially hedged international developed equity markets allows marginally different return assumptions to produce dramatic swings in optimal allocations.

Establishing permissible deviations from equilibrium weights helps control, but by no means solves, the problem of forecast accuracy. Using such a tactic to preserve diversification is simply a necessary expression of humility.

    ▨ *The simulation solution.* In confronting a problem shrouded in so much uncertainty, a problem in which inaccurate return forecasts can have a profound impact on the apparent solution, simulation is an indispensable tool. Although certainly not a panacea, a simulation illustrates the implications of a myriad of forecast combinations. It can reveal the forecast ranges implied by an existing strategic mix and can highlight ranges within which forecast changes will not significantly alter the optimal portfolio. Perhaps the main value of a simulation is simply that it provides much-needed perspective.

The following simulation incorporates approximately 3,500 expected return combinations and more than 5,000 different portfolios consisting of U.S., the partially hedged international developed market, and emerging market equity. A reasonably conservative assumption was made regarding the covariance matrix, which is detailed in Table 2.4. Because of the portfolio equivalence and corner solution issues associated with mean–variance analysis,[8] this simulation evaluates portfolios from a "relevant region" when measuring the benefit of international diversification. This region, highlighted in Figure 2.3, includes all portfolios offering some combination of higher return and lower risk than a U.S. equity portfolio.[9] Obviously, all the portfolios in this region are not efficient per se, but taken together, they offer a conservative estimate of the benefit of international diversification that reflects opportunities for both volatility reduction and return enhancement and that is insulated to some extent from the difficulties arising from the combination of the precision of mean–variance analysis and analysts' inability to generate accurate inputs.

The simulation results presented in Figure 2.4 and Figure 2.5 highlight three main points to bear in mind when constructing a global equity portfolio. First, international diversification is not an all-or-nothing proposition between developed market or emerging market equities. The two markets work together in delivering diversification benefits to U.S. investors. The strength of the forecast in one market bolsters the attractiveness of the other. For example, in Panel A of Figure 2.5, an expected 200 bp underperformance in the international developed markets relative to the U.S. equity market, combined with a 300 bp return premium in the emerging markets, still results in a 20 percent position in the international developed markets. In effect, the emerging market premium creates the opportunity to take advantage of the risk-reducing benefit of international developed markets without sacrificing return relative to a U.S. equity portfolio.

---

[8] Portfolio equivalence concerns the problem of a very different portfolio that lies, say, only 10 bps below the frontier portfolio and whether the difference between the two is meaningful, which is a particularly important question given the presence of forecast errors. The corner solution is the tendency of mean–variance analysis, given the presumed accuracy of inputs, to recommend large positions in a small subset of available assets. For a more thorough examination of these issues, see Landes and Gorman (1997).

[9] Some analyses have used the minimum-variance portfolio to illustrate the benefit of international equity. Although this approach is analytically convenient because it avoids the return issue, in practice, investors obviously must make statements regarding returns. With respect to the question at hand, the minimum-variance portfolio is neither theoretically optimal (unless returns are all equal) nor consistent with the volatility tolerance implied by the basis of comparison—a U.S. equity portfolio.

Table 2.4. Equity Simulation Inputs

Measure	United States	50% Hedged International Developed	Emerging
Expected return[a]	12.1%	Simulated	Simulated
Standard deviation[b]	16.8%	16.8%	24.9%
Correlation[b]			
United States	1.00		
International developed	0.60	1.00	
Emerging	0.37	0.50	1.00

[a]Thirty-five year expected return on the S&P 500 Index (January 1962 to December 1996).
[b]The U.S. and international developed market inputs are based on the January 1978–December 1996 data in Table 2.2. Because the IFC Investable Composite Index begins only in 1989, time-period-consistent emerging market statistics required some extrapolation using IFC Global country indexes.

Sources: Based on data from Standard & Poor's Corporation, MSCI, and the IFC.

Figure 2.3. Evaluation of Simulation Output: The Relevant Region

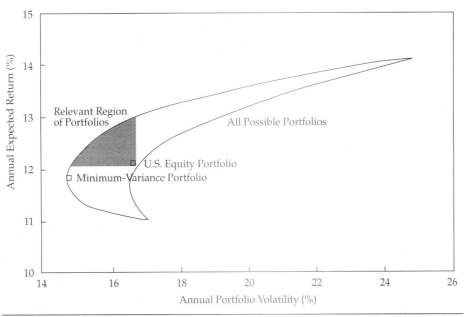

Note: Assumes return premium of –1.0 percent for international developed markets and 2.0 percent for emerging markets.

Figure 2.4. Sensitivity of Expected Return Improvement and Expected Volatility Reduction to Return Forecasts

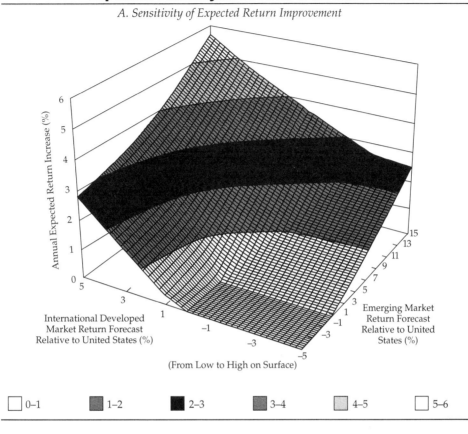

A. Sensitivity of Expected Return Improvement

| ☐ 0–1 | ▨ 1–2 | ■ 2–3 | ▨ 3–4 | ▨ 4–5 | ☐ 5–6 |

The second point is that, although the expected return improvement depicted in Panel A of Figure 2.4 is the focus of many investors, the imprecision of return forecasts renders questionable the expected performance enhancement of a few hundred basis points—let alone the 25 or 50 bps that often fall out of portfolio optimizations. Fortunately, the expected reduction in portfolio volatility depicted in Panel B of Figure 2.4 is a function of relatively more predictable inputs. Too often, however, tenuous return forecasts divert attention from this valuable benefit. Consider the 175 bp reduction in annual standard deviation associated with moving from a U.S. equity portfolio to an optimally diversified global equity portfolio when the return forecasts for the three equity markets are equal. (In Panel B, declines in the volatility-reduction benefit at higher return forecasts reflect the fact that the simulation is isolating

Figure 2.4. (continued)

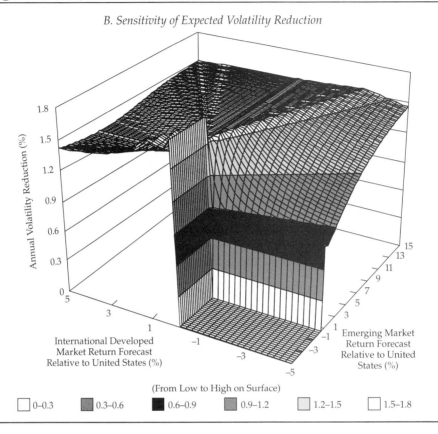

B. Sensitivity of Expected Volatility Reduction

(From Low to High on Surface)

☐ 0–0.3   ▨ 0.3–0.6   ■ 0.6–0.9   ▨ 0.9–1.2   ▨ 1.2–1.5   ☐ 1.5–1.8

a combination of risk improvement and return improvement, so some volatility reduction may be sacrificed in favor of additional return.) The global equity portfolio raises the lower bound of a five-year 95 percent confidence interval by 150 bps a year.[10] For a $100 million portfolio, this change is equivalent to

[10]The bounds of the 95 percent confidence interval for annualized return are defined as

$$e^{\left(m \pm 1.96\frac{s}{\sqrt{T}}\right)} - 1,$$

where

$$s = \sqrt{\ln\left[1+\left(\frac{\sigma}{1+\mu}\right)^2\right]}$$

$$m = \ln[1+\mu] - \frac{s^2}{2}$$

T = number of years

(where μ is the expected annual portfolio return and σ is the associated standard deviation).

Figure 2.5. Sensitivity of International Developed Market Allocation and Emerging Market Allocation to Return Forecasts

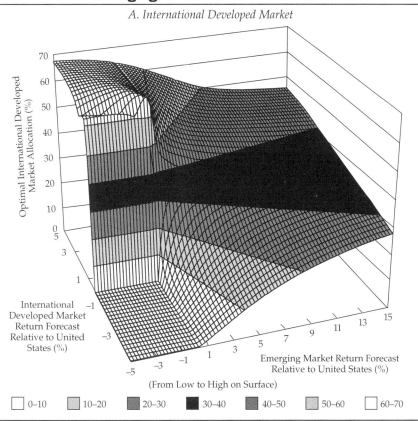

A. International Developed Market

(From Low to High on Surface)

☐ 0–10   ▨ 10–20   ▨ 20–30   ■ 30–40   ▨ 40–50   ▨ 50–60   ☐ 60–70

a $7 million reduction in value at risk (VAR) over a five-year period.[11] In the case of a strategic portfolio to be evaluated *ex post* on the basis of both absolute and risk-adjusted total return, perhaps the most significant *ex ante* contribution is to reduce the uncertainty of the outcome in a return-conscious manner.

The third point highlighted by the simulation results is that wide ranges in optimal international equity allocations are a function of trivial differences among return forecasts. Depending on the return forecasts, as summarized in

---

[11] Although VAR is typically used for much shorter horizons, it provides interesting perspective in strategic work. VAR is defined in this particular case as the minimum expected shortfall relative to expected portfolio appreciation over a five-year period at a 95 percent probability level and is calculated as the expected change in portfolio value over five years minus 1.65 (standard deviation of value changes).

Figure 2.5.   (continued)

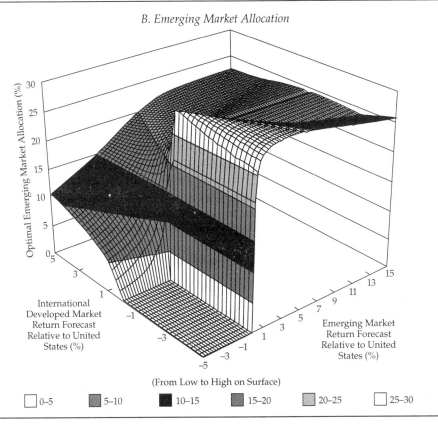

B. Emerging Market Allocation

(From Low to High on Surface)

☐ 0–5   ▨ 5–10   ■ 10–15   ▨ 15–20   ▨ 20–25   ☐ 25–30

Table 2.5, optimal international equity allocations range from zero to 67 percent for international developed markets and from zero to 29 percent for emerging markets. The surface area in Panel A of Figure 2.5 demonstrates that, given the relevant-region criteria, the recommended international allocation is zero if the equity markets in both international developed and emerging economies are expected to underperform the U.S. equity market by only 25 bps per year. Assume, however, that partially hedged international developed markets will outperform the United States by 25 bps and then the recommended international equity allocation jumps to almost 70 percent.

Because such minute expected-performance differentials can justify significant changes in non-U.S. allocations, return forecasts are the most consequential statements made in developing a policy mix. (The possible willingness of some plan sponsors to sacrifice some expected return—e.g., 25–50 bps relative to a U.S. equity portfolio—in exchange for a significant reduction in

Table 2.5.   Critical Return Forecasts for the Simulation

Portfolio	Portfolio Weights			Return Premium over U.S. Market		Improvement in:	
	United States	International Developed	Emerging	International Developed	Emerging	Return	Volatility
1	100.0%	0%	0%	−0.3%	−0.3%	0%	0%
2	79.0	0	21.0	−0.3	0	0	0.8
3	57.0	14.1	28.8	−0.3	0.3	0	1.1
4	50.0	50.0	0	0	−0.3	0	1.8
5	41.5	39.6	18.9	0	0	0	1.7
6	39.2	36.7	24.1	0	0.3	0.1	1.5
7	22.3	67.0	10.7	0.3	−0.3	0.1	1.4
8	21.1	63.5	15.4	0.3	0	0.2	1.4
9	25.2	54.1	20.6	0.3	0.3	0.2	1.4
Range	21–100%	0–67%	0–29%	+/−25 bps	+/−25 bps	—	—

expected annual volatility does not change this point.) As the surface areas in Figure 2.5 illustrate, correct forecasts of positive or negative performance differentials have far more bearing on the proper positioning of the strategic portfolio than does the size of the forecast errors.

The focus thus returns to the essence of the strategic portfolio problem. Statements regarding the direction of performance differentials have a tremendous effect on the optimal strategic asset mix, yet investors know too little about the future to make such statements with much confidence. Although historical performance for developed equity markets has been very similar over time,[12] investors do not know for certain that this observation will hold in the future. Even if such an equilibrium does unequivocally hold, no way exists to determine how many years will be required to substantiate this view. Furthermore, even if returns were similar over a reasonably long period, they will not be identical, and whether or not performance differences will be sufficient to cover cost differences is impossible to know today. The only statement that carries any degree of confidence is that the return difference between U.S. and international developed equity markets probably will be large enough over a single strategic planning period to render cost a moot point.

Global Equity Allocation. The point of examining the daunting aspects of the strategic portfolio problem is not to obviate the need to make forecasts but, rather, to instill the appropriate respect for the difficulty of the problem and

---

[12] For example, Siegel (1994) points out that, despite wars and other exogenous events, the average real total return in the U.S., U.K., and German equity markets over the 1926–92 period was between 5.5 and 6.5 percent. (Although Siegel does not mention it explicitly, the long-term average return in Japan also appears to fall within this range.)

to generate the necessary skepticism regarding the accuracy of any forecast. Such skepticism creates the proper bias toward diversification and shifts the focus to the task of establishing appropriate global equity allocation ranges.

Table 2.6 highlights the areas in Figure 2.4 and Figure 2.5 associated with some common relative-return forecasts.[13] These return premiums should be regarded as net of incremental passive costs (relative to U.S. equity) for indexed portfolios and net of incremental active costs plus the expected alpha for actively managed portfolios. (The adjustment for expected value added is necessary to make the comparison between active and passive management a fair one; after all, no plan sponsor pays active-management fees for passive performance.) In the case of actively managed portfolios, the incremental cost estimate is 77 bps for international developed market equity and 220 bps for emerging market equity.[14] In the case of indexed portfolios, lower security turnover and the use of futures contracts reduce these costs significantly.

Given the reasonably conservative covariance-matrix assumption in Table 2.4 and some common return-premium forecasts, the simulation recommends a substantial international equity commitment. An analysis of the data in Table 2.6 leads to the following appropriate global equity allocation ranges as a percentage of a global equity portfolio and a portfolio with 60 percent equity:

	Global Equity Portfolio	60 Percent Equity Portfolio
U.S. equity	30–50%	18–30%
International developed market equity	30–45	18–27
Emerging market equity	20–25	12–15

These allocation ranges are quite aggressive, particularly for emerging markets, relative to the 84–15–1 ratio of assets (U.S. to international developed to emerging equity markets) held by the average U.S. pension portfolio and are likely to be unpalatable to most plan sponsors. Behavioral finance posits

---

[13]Strategic return forecasts for the developed markets tend to be based heavily on cyclical factors. Variation in the specification and projection of such factors leads to a lack of consensus on the expected performance differential, so both positive and negative forecasts are presented. Conversely, strategic return forecasts for the emerging markets have a large secular component, which produces a positively skewed set of expectations. The secular argument is that emerging markets are typified by an inexpensive labor force, young population, cheap land, high savings rate, and increasingly stimulative government policies (e.g., privatization and monetary, fiscal, and regulatory reform) and that, ultimately, these factors initiate an emerging market investment cycle: Appropriate policies bolster investor confidence, which results in capital inflow (in the form of foreign demand for stocks and bonds and, most importantly, foreign direct investment), high real GDP growth, and significant stock price appreciation. These results validate government directives, and the cycle thus becomes self-perpetuating.
[14]The incremental cost estimate is addressed in Chapter 4.

Table 2.6.   Some Common Return Forecasts for the Simulation

Portfolio	Recommended Portfolio Weights			Return Premium over U.S.		Improvement in:	
	United States	International Developed	Emerging	International Developed	Emerging	Return	Volatility
1	49.7%	23.1%	27.2%	−1.0%	2.0%	0.3%	1.4%
2	46.5	27.9	25.7	−1.0	3.0	0.5	1.5
3	45.0	30.5	24.5	−1.0	4.0	0.7	1.5
4	39.2	36.7	24.1	0	2.0	0.5	1.5
5	39.2	36.7	24.1	0	3.0	0.7	1.5
6	39.2	36.7	24.1	0	4.0	1.0	1.5
7	30.2	47.3	22.5	1.0	2.0	0.9	1.5
8	32.2	45.1	22.7	1.0	3.0	1.1	1.5
9	33.3	43.8	22.9	1.0	4.0	1.4	1.5

the following three explanations for this aversion (only the last of which provides an arguably acceptable basis for adjusting the allocation ranges derived from Table 2.6):

▪ *Biased expectations.* The performance of equity markets in the 1990s, coupled with stories in the press contrasting the resurgent global competitiveness of U.S. companies with the turmoil in Asia, has led many investors to be overconfident regarding the likelihood of the United States continuing to outperform international developed and emerging equity markets over the next few years. The historical perspective on the U.S. equity market provided in Figure 2.6, however, puts recent U.S. performance in context. The disequilibrium that has the U.S. equity market as both the high-return and low-volatility alternative cannot persist indefinitely. The reward-to-variability ratio, which is return divided by standard deviation, has not reached a level as high as December 1996 in 30 years, and this ratio has demonstrated a strong tendency to revert to the mean.

▪ *Reference dependence.* Because the reference point of most U.S. investors is a U.S. equity portfolio, an asymmetry exists in what investors consider a tolerable mistake. The rolling three-year historical optimizations in Table 2.3 show that as many periods occurred in which owning only international equity was optimal as occurred in which U.S. equity was the best choice. Having a 20 percent international equity stake during a period when a 100 percent international position is optimal raises the blood pressure of few U.S. investors. Owning a 20 percent stake abroad when a 100 percent U.S. equity allocation is optimal, however, results in grumbling about the benefits of international diversification. In other words, the regret associated with having 20 percent unexposed to a strong U.S. equity market is greater than

Figure 2.6.   U.S. Stock Returns, January 1946–December 1996

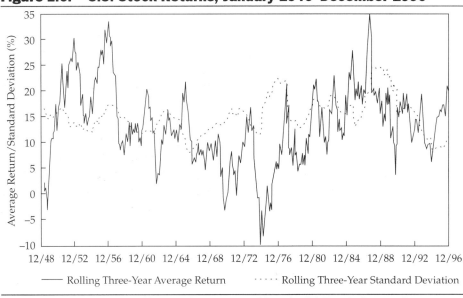

Source: Based on data from Ibbotson Associates and Standard & Poor's Corporation.

the regret associated with having 80 percent unexposed to a strong international equity market.

   ▨   *Agency concerns.* The fear of deviating from commonly held principles and benchmarks may perpetuate suboptimal investment decisions. If plan sponsors deviate from conventional wisdom and suffer an adverse outcome, the repercussions in terms of litigation, job security, or performance evaluation can be serious. The industry preoccupation with peer-group performance comparisons testifies to this concern. As a result of such agency issues, diversification beyond the level of other pension plans is not viewed as a costless undertaking and risk aversion with respect to international equity is not constant. In other words, as Peter Bernstein discerned from "Pascal's Wager" (named after 17th century French mathematician and philosopher Blaise Pascal's famous analysis of the problem of "betting" on the existence of God), the *consequences* of being wrong must dominate the *probability* of being wrong.[15]

   An Expanded Simulation. Although investment professionals can debate whether or not agency issues *should* affect the portfolio construction process, they must acknowledge that, in practice, such concerns *do* play a role.

[15]*Against the Gods: The Remarkable Story of Risk* (New York: John Wiley & Sons, 1996):69–71.

To address this problem, the initial simulation must be expanded. The recommended portfolios derived from the data in Figure 2.5 are simply a function of the initial covariance-matrix assumption in Table 2.4 and a given set of expected returns. This line of analysis assumes the level of risk aversion is constant and is focused only on the stochastic, or probabilistic, aspect of the portfolio construction problem. For each of the 3,500 expected return combinations considered jointly with the given covariance matrix, however, a plan sponsor could experience a myriad of potential outcomes, both in return and in covariance structure, over a single strategic planning period of five years.

To understand how, consider Portfolio 4 in Table 2.6, which assumes no difference in developed market returns and a 200 bp emerging market return premium. In Figure 2.7, the range of possible outcomes is depicted by the shaded area that surrounds the actual assumptions, which are denoted by the small nonagon (solid white line). For example, the expected 14 percent emerg-

Figure 2.7. Potential Input Combinations over One Strategic Planning Period

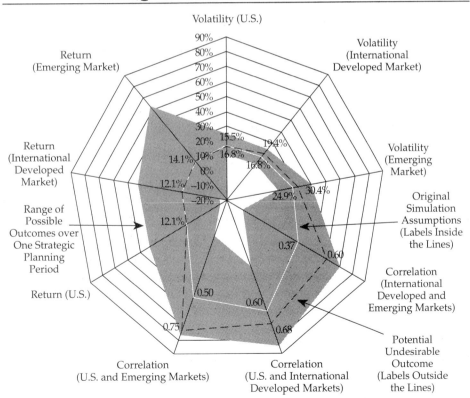

ing market return could translate into a *realized* five-year annualized return between –20 percent and 63 percent.[16] Similarly, the expected 0.60 correlation between the United States and international developed equity markets could produce a *realized* five-year correlation between 0.28 and 0.84.

In the context of rising risk aversion associated with the international equity allocation, this range of possible outcomes, specifically the observation that the potential outcome distribution may have negative consequences for the plan sponsor, warrants special attention. The impact of poor relative international equity returns on the recommended portfolio should be clear from the data in Figure 2.5. The initial simulation, however, did not vary correlations or standard deviations, so Table 2.7 focuses on the effect of a very undesirable and low-probability (given the population parameters) covariance-matrix outcome. This outcome is indicated in Figure 2.7 by the mid-sized nonagon (dashed line). Relative to the recommended portfolios in Table 2.6, which reflect the same return assumptions, the allocation to international developed markets in Table 2.7 drops by an average of 65 percent and the allocation to emerging markets falls by an average of 94 percent. The covariance-matrix effect may be less extreme than the expected-return effect, but all other things being equal, the covariance-matrix effect can have a significant effect on the recommended international equity allocation.

Table 2.7. Effect of Undesirable Covariance-Matrix Outcome

	Recommended Portfolio Weights			Return Premium over U.S.		Improvement in:	
Portfolio	United States	International Developed	Emerging	International Developed	Emerging	Return	Volatility
1	97.0%	2.0%	1.0%	–1.0%	2.0%	0%	0%
2	93.2	4.9	1.9	–1.0	3.0	0	0
3	91.5	6.4	2.1	–1.0	4.0	0	0
4	83.0	15.8	1.2	0	2.0	0	0.1
5	83.0	15.8	1.2	0	3.0	0	0.1
6	83.0	15.8	1.2	0	4.0	0	0.1
7	77.2	21.5	1.3	1.0	2.0	0.2	0.1
8	78.1	20.5	1.4	1.0	3.0	0.2	0.1
9	78.7	19.9	2.4	1.0	4.0	0.3	0.1

---

[16]As painful as it has been, the Asian crisis of the 1990s has been completely consistent with this expectation. Significant risks accompany emerging market investing—ranging from political and expropriation risk to the risk that a market could be overwhelmed by the capital flows brought about by liberalization. The widths of the potential outcome ranges in Figure 2.7 reflect these risks.

For each set of original assumptions (i.e., the given covariance matrix and one of the 3,500 expected return combinations—hereafter referred to as the population parameters), this exercise was repeated for each of the 5,000 nonagons that constitute the universe of potential outcomes. The recommended portfolio generated by the initial simulation is the simple average of the recommended portfolios associated with each of those 5,000 scenarios. In the expanded simulation, however, the result is different. Assuming that the plan sponsor utility function is such that negative potential outcomes (those that make a plan sponsor look bad relative to some peer group) reduce utility more than favorable potential outcomes increase it, the expanded simulation introduces a penalty function that reduces the recommended international exposure relative to the results of the initial simulation. This approach penalizes possible outcomes by the magnitude of the undesirable deviation from a normal institutional portfolio on both an absolute and a risk-adjusted return basis.

In the expanded simulation, the recommended portfolio for a given expected return combination is determined by an average of the 5,000 potential portfolios weighted by the penalty factor.[17] Clearly, such an adjustment is largely a return-driven process, but the covariance matrix has an influence through its impact on risk-adjusted performance. For example, a higher-than-average international equity allocation over a period when global equity returns are similar but international equity return volatility is relatively high will adversely affect the risk-adjusted-performance ranking of the plan within its universe. Such an outcome is undesirable and, therefore, is penalized.

The expanded simulation yields the following recommended allocation ranges—once again, for a global equity portfolio and a portfolio with 60 percent equity. Note that the international component in each case exceeds that of the typical institutional portfolio:

	Global Equity Portfolio		60 Percent Equity Portfolio	
	Typical	Recommended	Typical	Recommended
U.S. equity	84%	45–70%	50%	27–42%
International developed market equity	15	25–40	9	15–24
Emerging market equity	1	5–15	1	3–9

Obviously, these results are contingent on the range of return combinations considered, the covariance-matrix assumptions, and the definition of the penalty function and normal portfolio. The need to specify the population

---

[17] Given the nebulous quality of disutility, experiments with several specifications of the penalty function precedes the recommendations. Information about these experiments is available from the author.

parameter and utility function contributes significantly to the inescapable uncertainty investors endeavor to manage, but no definitive answers exist in these areas—only well-reasoned approaches and recommendations. By using simulations and conservative assumptions, an investment manager can systematically derive strategic allocation ranges in a manner consistent with the practical considerations of plan sponsors and the diversification necessitated by the enormous uncertainty surrounding the future performance of the markets. A plan sponsor can then use current strategic forecasts to determine where the actual policy allocations should fall within the ranges.[18]

Finally, because the expanded simulation reduces the international equity allocation recommended by the initial analysis, the diversification consequence of that decision is worth mentioning. Figure 2.8 illustrates the diminishing marginal diversification benefit associated with moving from a U.S. equity portfolio to a minimum-variance portfolio containing 43 percent international developed markets and 9 percent emerging markets. (The minimum-variance portfolio is used as a simple illustration of the concept of diminishing marginal benefit in which incremental return is not a consideration, but the same dynamic is at work in each of the myriad of relevant ranges generated by the simulation). As Figure 2.8 shows, at an allocation of 10 percent international developed markets and 6 percent emerging markets, half of the almost 200 bp volatility reduction relative to a U.S. equity portfolio is captured. At an allocation of 19 percent international developed and 8 percent emerging, three-quarters of the diversification benefit is realized. In a world in which the consequences of assuming additional international equity exposure do not change, this point is irrelevant. If ERISA (Employee Retirement Income Security Act of 1974)-related standards of prudence or the prominence of peer performance comparisons attach potentially negative consequences to additional exposure, however, an important insight for investors is to understand that the price of imposing *reasonable* limitations is not extraordinarily high.

The Tactical Case for International Equity

Tactical views supplement the strategic views to ensure that a portfolio remains on course to meet its investment objectives. Because generating strategic views is a process fraught with uncertainties, the TAA process (i.e., periodic adjustments to the strategic portfolio that are driven by prevailing market conditions) is an essential means of incorporating additional information into the investment management process to mitigate potential vulnerabilities in the policy mix. To make the tactical case for international diversification, two

---

[18] The appendix addresses how alternative assets and liabilities affect the recommendations in this monograph.

Figure 2.8. Marginal Diversification Benefit of International Equity

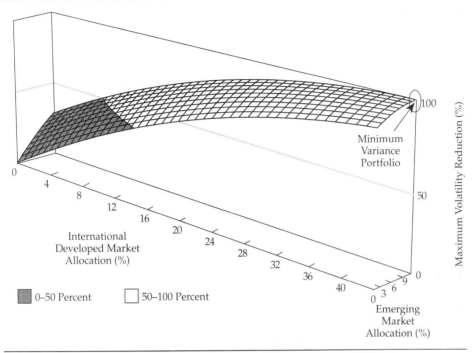

Note: Minimum variance portfolio is based on the simulation inputs in Table 2.4.

conditions must exist. First, the financial marketplace must offer an attractive opportunity set, and second, an investment manager must possess the means to capitalize on those opportunities.

The Opportunity Set. From 1978 through 1996, the return differences among the developed equity markets were huge, as shown in Figure 2.9. Given a 50 percent hedge ratio, thousands of basis points separated the best-performing market from the worst during each year of this period, and 1995 was the only year in which the United States was the top-performing equity market. Further, with the exception of the incredible performance streak of Hong Kong during the early 1990s, considerable variation occurred in the best- and worst-performing markets from one year to the next. When emerging markets are included, as in Figure 2.10, the return differentials become even more dramatic; tens of thousands of basis points regularly separated the best- and worst-performing markets. Hence, the active manager with the freedom to move among the equity markets of the world enjoys a wealth of opportunities to add value to a portfolio.

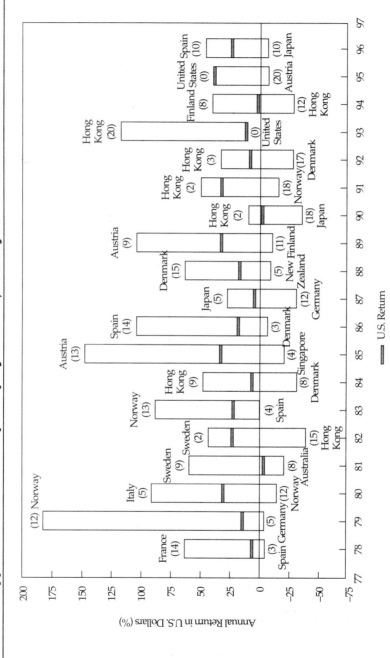

Gorman

Figure 2.9. Opportunities in Developed Equity Markets, January 1978–December 1996

Note: 50 percent hedged returns. Numbers in parentheses denote number of countries returning less than (bottom) and more than (top) the United States.

Source: Based on MSCI data.

Figure 2.10. Opportunities in the Global Equity Market, January 1978–December 1996

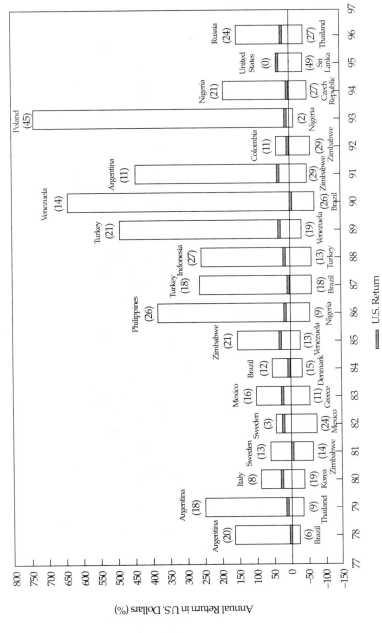

Note: 50 percent hedged returns for developed markets; unhedged returns for emerging markets. Numbers in parentheses denote number of countries returning less than (bottom) and more than (top) the United States.

Source: Based on data from MSCI and the IFC.

The Means. A systematic, quantitative approach incorporating multifactor models that explain even a small portion of return variance can capture added value through country and currency selection. In addition, the dynamic nature of capital markets requires a qualitative component in the decision-making process, because the perspectives of portfolio managers and analysts are indispensable in assessing the continued relevance of factors in the quantitative models and in identifying emerging factors to test in the models.

Numerous approaches exist for generating the return estimates that ultimately drive the tactical shifts in portfolios. The following models provide two examples. The first model is a regression-based multifactor approach to forecasting equity market returns. This model incorporates a valuation measure, an interest rate factor, an inflation factor, an economic factor, and a technical/sentiment indicator, and it captures nonlinearities indirectly through variable specification. Note that the idiosyncrasies of global equity markets, both in terms of market structure and the behavior of the marginal price setter, prevent the rote application of identical factors to all markets. Even the specification and significance of virtually universal factors, such as valuation measures, vary widely among equity markets.

The second model is a CART (classification and regression tree)-based multifactor approach to forecasting currency market returns, as represented in Figure 2.11. This model incorporates a variety of technical factors and captures nonlinearities directly through the tree structure. CART models are unique to a particular currency, as are the equity models.

Signals from the two approaches are combined in a portfolio construction algorithm to determine the appropriate adjustments to make to the strategic portfolio. Highly cost-effective futures contracts represent the preferred means of adjusting equity market exposures.[19]

Beyond Conventional Performance Benchmarks. Despite possessing some long-term theoretical merit, the country weights in popular international return indexes have not proven to be optimal per se over a single strategic planning period. At a minimum, plan sponsors should consider assuming policy-setting responsibility for allocations to large international equity markets, such as Germany, France, Japan, and the United Kingdom. After all, for even a modest international equity commitment, exposures to these countries as a percentage of total plan assets often are as large, or larger, than other positions that receive policy-level attention (e.g., cash, real estate, high-yield bonds, private equity). Moving beyond the conventional benchmarks to capitalize on tactical information, to incorporate strategic views, or simply to focus on a manageable number of countries is an important step that

---

[19]Chapter 4 provides a more detailed discussion of the advantage of futures contracts.

Figure 2.11. A CART Approach

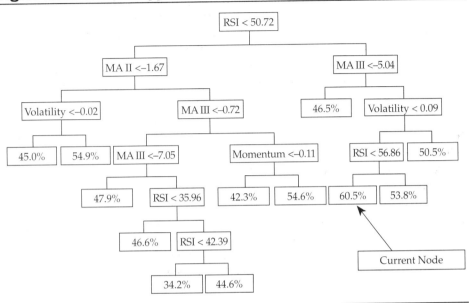

Note: MA = moving average; RSI = relative strength index. "Current" levels are

MA I	0.69
MA II	0.01
MA III	1.74
Volatility	0.03
RSI	56.30
Momentum	0.15

can be accomplished in a manner sensitive to the widespread institutional adherence to these indexes.

Consider the non-U.S. portion of the MSCI All Country (AC) World Index in Table 2.8. In the absence of strategic views suggesting otherwise, the benchmark should be adjusted to emphasize the Japanese, German, French, and U.K. stock markets.[20] Along with the United States, these countries are the cornerstone of the global economy, and their equity markets are among the most developed and well diversified (e.g., low company and sector concentration) in the world. Not surprisingly then, the covariance matrix for international equity returns is such that these core markets can be emphasized with only modest tracking error relative to the MSCI AC World Index and without diminishing the diversification appeal of international equity. Most important, liquid futures contracts in these markets allow large institutions to manage their key country exposures in a cost-effective manner.

---

[20]The appendix contains further discussion of the major equity market issue.

Table 2.8.   MSCI AC World Index Weights, December 1996
(excluding the United States)

Europe, Africa, and Middle East		Asia and Far East		Americas	
Country	Weight	Country	Weight	Country	Weight
United Kingdom	16.0%	Japan	26.9%	Canada	4.0%
Germany	6.8	Hong Kong	3.1	Brazil	2.6
France	5.8	Australia	2.5	Mexico	2.1
Switzerland	4.7	Taiwan	2.3	Chile	0.5
Netherlands	3.9	Malaysia	2.2	Argentina	0.4
Italy	2.6	South Korea	1.1	Venezuela	0.1
Sweden	2.1	Singapore	1.1	Peru	0.1
Spain	1.9	Indonesia	0.7	Colombia	0.1
South Africa	1.4	India	0.7		
Belgium	1.0	Thailand	0.6		
Denmark	0.7	Philippines	0.5		
Finland	0.6	New Zealand	0.3		
Norway	0.5	Pakistan	0.1		
Austria	0.3	China	0.1		
Ireland	0.3	Sri Lanka	0		
Israel	0.3				
Portugal	0.3				
Turkey	0.2				
Czech Republic	0.2				
Greece	0.2				
Poland	0.1				
Hungary	0.1				
Jordan	0				
Total	49.7%		42.3%		7.9%

Alternative Benchmark I in Table 2.9 facilitates the goal of using the TAA process to incorporate additional information into the investment management process. The control over the key country exposures provided by this approach is ample compensation for the tracking error relative to a conventional index. The four core markets should play an expanded role in an international equity portfolio because of their significance, liquidity, size, sophistication, historical records, and relative stability. The allocations to the core markets should not be an artifact of some index construction methodology. In short, having high-quality forecasts on 75 percent of the portfolio is preferable to having high-quality insights on 56 percent of the portfolio and relatively little or no insight on the remaining 44 percent.

34

Table 2.9. Comparison of Alternative Benchmarks with MSCI AC World Index, as of December 1996

Country	MSCI AC World Index			Alternative Benchmark I			Alternative Benchmark II		
	Total	Emerging	Developed	Total	Emerging	Developed	Total	Emerging	Developed
Core									
United Kingdom	16%			25%			25%		
Germany	7			13			13		
France	6			13			13		
Japan	27			25			25		
Core total	56%			75%			75%		
Non-core									
Americas	8%	4%	4%	4%	2%	2%	4%	4%	0%
Europe, Africa, and Middle East	21	3	19	12	1	10	8	0	8
Asia and Far East	15	8	7	9	5	4	13	8	4
Non-core total	44%	15%	30%	25%	8%	17%	25%	13%	13%
Trading bloc[a]									
EMU	23%			31%			27%		
AFTA	5			3			4		
NAFTA	5			3			0		

Note: Columns may not add to totals because of rounding.

[a] With EMU rapidly approaching, trading bloc exposure is an additional way of assessing benchmark structure. The EMU (European Monetary Union) total represents the likely first round entrants: Germany, France, Italy, Spain, the Netherlands, Belgium, Austria, Finland, Portugal, and Ireland. Luxembourg is not represented in the MSCI AC World Index, and Sweden, Denmark, Greece, and the United Kingdom are possible second round entrants. The total for AFTA (or ASEAN—Association of Southeast Asian Nations) represents Indonesia, Malaysia, the Philippines, Singapore, and Thailand. Brunei Darussalam, Vietnam, Laos, and Myanmar are not represented in the index. The NAFTA (North American Free Trade Agreement) total is for Canada and Mexico.

Alternative Benchmark I represents a starting point and does not reflect strategic views. In practice, the benchmark is refined in a diversification-minded manner by balancing the information content of the strategic forecasts and the information provided by the tactical process. For example, strategic considerations might justify a high emerging markets allocation, but tactical considerations might suggest tempering this increase. Although the inefficiencies associated with less-integrated markets may present attractive opportunities, the combination of high transaction costs, the liquidity required by institutional investors, and the challenges facing a quantitative investment process limit the ability to capitalize on these opportunities.

Figure 2.12 illustrates the tracking-error consequences of adjusting the MSCI AC World Index. As the capitalization-weighted allocation to the core markets increases, the alternative benchmark reaches a point at which tracking error is zero (i.e., the index is replicated). To the left of this point, the cap-weighted allocation to the core markets produces a lower tracking error than the simpler, equal-weighted approach. The roles switch, however, as the allocation to the core markets exceeds 70 percent. This change reflects the fact that a combination of the French, German, and U.K. equity markets has a higher correlation than Japan with the remainder of the MSCI AC World Index because of the prominence of such European countries as Switzerland, the Netherlands, and Italy.

Figure 2.12. Tracking-Error Consequences of Benchmark Adjustments

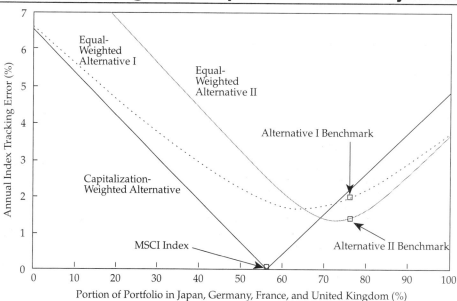

Source: Based on return data from MSCI.

Table 2.10 demonstrates that Alternative Benchmark I offers diversification benefits almost identical to those associated with the MSCI AC World Index. For example, the correlation between Alternative Benchmark I and the United States is 0.59. The correlation between the MSCI AC World Index and the United States is 0.57. The difference is trivial.

Alternative Benchmark II illustrates that concentrating the non-core component of the composite in only 12 equal-weighted countries can significantly reduce the tracking error associated with Alternative Benchmark I. This simple approach eliminates the many tiny index exposures to markets that cannot easily accommodate institutional positions and that portfolio managers often disregard anyway. The point is not to dismiss the other 30 countries but rather to demonstrate that, without undesirable diversification or peer-group comparison consequences, a plan sponsor can play an active role in establishing international equity policy allocations and, in doing so, can move beyond grudging acceptance of the country weights falling out of conventional return indexes.

Table 2.10. Diversification Implications of Alternative Benchmarks, January 1993–December 1997

	Conventional MSCI AC World Index	Alternative Benchmark I[a]	Alternative Benchmark II[a]
Correlation between:			
Core and non-core[b]	0.71	0.79	0.75
Core and United States	0.47	0.55	0.55
Non-core and United States	0.60	0.60	0.53
Composite and United States	0.57	0.59	0.58
MSCI and alternative	2.00	0.99	0.99
Measure			
Volatility (U.S. = 13.0%)	14.2%	13.5%	14.0%
Tracking error[c]	0 %	2.0%	1.4%

Note: Date range is a result of emerging market data availability.

[a]Statistics generated by bootstrapping five years of monthly 50 percent hedged developed market returns and unhedged emerging market returns.

[b]Core represents the composite component of France, Germany, Japan, and the United Kingdom. Non-core represents (for Alternative Benchmark I) cap-weighted allocations to the remaining 42 countries and (for Alternative Benchmark II) equal-weighted allocations to only 12 countries: Argentina, Australia, Brazil, Hong Kong, Indonesia, Italy, Korea, Malaysia, Norway, Sweden, Switzerland, and Taiwan.

[c]Tracking error $= \sum_{i=1}^{n} \sum_{j=1}^{n} (w_{Alternative} - w_{Index})_i (w_{Alternative} - w_{Index})_j \sigma_{ij}$, where w is weight in country i or j and σ_{ij} is covariance between countries i and j.

Summary

Over a strategic planning period, prudent portfolio management requires using as many reliable information sources as possible. Strategic asset allocation cannot be considered in isolation. Because of the low confidence that investors can assign to differences in long-term return forecasts, optimizing among the many international equity markets requires establishing a myriad of constraints and wrestling with portfolio equivalence issues. Both strategic and tactical considerations must be combined in a manner consistent with the errors associated with the information set of each and with the objectives and constraints of the portfolio. The alternative benchmarks reflect these realities and provide the latitude to alleviate some of the strategic uncertainty via a cost-conscious, diversification-minded TAA process.

3. Benchmarking and Historical Perspective

One of the ironies in investment management is that many plan sponsors expend a great deal of effort arriving at a strategic U.S. equity allocation and then are content to lump all the other equity markets together in one or two aggregate international equity allocations, depending on how emerging markets are handled. This practice reflects two philosophical inconsistencies.

First, many plan sponsors argue that the problems with the international capital asset pricing model (ICAPM) prevent them from using it as a basis for determining the international allocation in a global equity portfolio, but their use of a market-capitalization-weighted international equity benchmark, which is premised on the ICAPM, represents an implicit endorsement of the theory.

The second inconsistency is that a constant-proportion allocation to the U.S. equity market is an inherently contrarian investment approach. In other words, when the U.S. market performs very well, rebalancing the portfolio requires liquidating some of the increased U.S. position. Conversely, the use of a market-capitalization-weighted international equity benchmark represents a trend-following investment approach. The exposure to markets that perform well increases over time, producing results such as the Japanese representation in the MSCI EAFE Index increasing from 30 percent in 1978 to more than 60 percent at the height of the bubble and then falling to 30 percent in 1996.

International Developed Market Equity Indexes

This discussion of the popular international developed market equity indexes will assist plan sponsors in meeting the following objectives:

- If an aggregate international equity benchmark is used, plan sponsors must understand the strategic statements implied by that benchmark regarding country, currency, sector, and company exposures.
- Plan sponsors must critically evaluate a myriad of studies done on the benefits of international equity. To assess properly the probable prospective contribution of international equity to a portfolio, they must understand the benchmarks used to represent historical performance.[1]

Morgan Stanley Capital International (MSCI) indexes are the most frequently used benchmarks and, for that reason, underlie most of the analyses in this monograph. Specifically, the MSCI EAFE (Europe/Australasia/Far

East) Index, a subcomponent of the MSCI World Index, has become synonymous with international equity returns.[2] Table 3.1 provides a performance snapshot for this benchmark relative to the U.S. equity market. Despite the popularity of the MSCI EAFE Index, plan sponsors often use the non-U.S. component of two alternative benchmarks—the Financial Times/Standard & Poor's Actuaries[3] World Index and the Salomon Smith Barney Broad Market Index compiled by the Salomon Smith Barney Equity Index Group.

The indexes of the three data providers vary in three ways—length of return history, breadth of coverage, and significance of adjustments for investability considerations—as summarized in Table 3.2 and Table 3.3. No single benchmark offers an ideal combination of these three attributes. The MSCI World Index offers the longest data history but includes only a sampling of companies and makes few investability adjustments. The FT/S&P Actuaries World Index (FT/S&P-AWI) includes more companies than the MSCI alternative, but its investability adjustments are similar and its return history shorter. The Salomon Smith Barney Broad Market Index (SSB BMI) offers the broadest coverage and makes the most comprehensive investability adjustments, but its data history is by far the shortest. The impact of SSB's investability adjustments for the BMI is evident in Table 3.3. Despite the fact that the BMI includes three times as many companies as FT/S&P-AWI (7,095 versus 2,232), its total index market capitalization is 10 percent smaller than that of FT/S&P-AWI ($11.8 trillion versus $13.1 trillion).

Several alternatives to market-cap weights are available that, primarily because of concerns about corporate cross-holding of stock, share the objective of reducing the representation of Japan, as shown in Table 3.4. For example, the FT/S&P Cross-Holding-Adjusted Index reduces the market capitalization of Japan by almost 50 percent and, within that market, dramatically reduces the representation of the finance sector. The free float averages only 25 percent of shares outstanding for banks, which lie at the heart of the

---

[1]Performance indexes are not static. Over time, index methodologies are revised and countries are added, transaction costs faced by managers in replicating the index (and dealing with index revisions) decline, and the industry composition of constituent countries changes. For example, not long ago Malaysia was primarily focused on agriculture; now it is industrial. Similarly, 20 years ago the technology sector in the United States was tiny compared with its current size.

[2]Data on the MSCI World Index (EAFE, United States, and Canada) are presented to put the EAFE Index, which is the focus of this section, in context. Because U.S. policy positions are typically determined independently, the EAFE Index is used far more frequently than the MSCI World Index.

[3]The FT/S&P Actuaries World indexes are owned by Financial Times Stock Exchange (FTSE) International; Goldman, Sachs & Company; and Standard & Poor's Corporation. FTSE and S&P compile the indexes in conjunction with the Faculty of Actuaries and the Institute of Actuaries.

Table 3.1. MSCI EAFE Index Annualized Performance Summary versus U.S. Equity Market

Period/Measurement	EAFE[a]	U.S. Equities
27 years (since inception, 1970–96)		
Average return[b]	14.5%	13.1%
Standard deviation[c]	19.3	17.0
19 years (1978–96)[d]		
Average return	16.8	16.8
Standard deviation	20.1	16.8
7 years (1990–96)		
Average return	5.4	15.7
Standard deviation	18.6	13.3
5 years (1992–96)		
Average return	9.5	16.0
Standard deviation	14.9	9.9

[a]Unhedged into U.S. dollars (conventional way of presenting EAFE returns).

[b]$E[R] = (1 + \mu_m)^{12} - 1$, where μ_m is the mean of monthly returns.

[c]$\sigma = \sqrt{[\sigma_m^2 + (1 + \mu_m)^2]^{12} - (1 + \mu_m)^{24}}$, where σ_m is the standard deviation of monthly returns. See Deborah Gunthorpe and Haim Levy, "Portfolio Composition and the Investment Horizon," *Financial Analysts Journal*, vol. 50, no. 1 (January/February 1994):51–56.

[d]In this monograph, the 19-year historical period (January 1978 to December 1996) is used for two comparability reasons: (1) January 1978 is the inception date of Putnam Investments Global Asset Allocation Group's hedged return series, and (2) unhedged returns from the first half of the 1970s do not reflect the current exchange rate system. The EAFE Index registered no currency returns during 1970 and most of 1971, because the Bretton Woods system was shaky but still in place. Not until 1973, following two major devaluations of the U.S. dollar, did major exchange rates begin to float freely. The 1976 Jamaica Agreement on revision of the Articles of Agreement of the International Monetary Fund formally endorsed floating exchange rates, the discontinuation of gold as a reserve asset, and greater IMF funding.

Source: MSCI.

keiretsu, or Japanese industrial complexes.

Note, however, that these alternative weighting schemes have some interesting implications for countries other than Japan. Consider the significance of Germany, Italy, and the United Kingdom in the MSCI GDP- and market-cap-weighted indexes.[4] In the GDP-weighted index, the weights are 20, 9, and 9 percent, respectively. In the market-cap-weighted index, the weights in these

---

[4]GDP-weighted benchmarks are contrarian in nature because changes in GDP are far less volatile than fluctuations in market capitalization. So, rebalancing to GDP weights typically involves taking profits in countries that have performed well and increasing positions in markets with lagging performance.

Table 3.2. Global Equity Benchmark Methodology Comparison

Index	Length of Return History	Breadth of Coverage	Adjustments to Market-Cap Weights
MSCI World Subindexes: No mutually exclusive large-cap and small-cap subindexes.[a]	Inception: 12/31/69	60 percent of total market cap for all industries.	MSCI considers liquidity, free float, and cross-holdings in selecting securities. Once selected, securities are typically included at full market cap (both listed and unlisted shares included).
FT/S&P Actuaries World[b] Subindexes: FT/S&P-AWI large cap (top 75 percent of market cap). FT/S&P-AWI medium-small cap (bottom 25 percent of market cap).	Inception: 12/31/85[c]	85 percent of available market cap as defined by some general investability screens, with consideration given to economic sector distribution.	FT/S&P excludes the bottom 5 percent of country market cap. If 25 percent or more of a security is publicly available, the issue is included at full market cap. Market cap is adjusted in the cases of securities subject to foreign ownership restrictions and large issues having only 10–25 percent free float. Government holdings are included unless these shares cannot legally be offered to the public.
SSB Broad Market Index (BMI) Subindexes: SSB Primary Market Index (PMI) (top 80 percent of market cap). SSB Extended Market Index (EMI) (bottom 20 percent of market cap).	Inception: 6/30/89	All companies with a market cap larger than $100 million.	SSB uses float-capitalization weights for each security. In other words, market cap is comprehensively adjusted for corporate cross-holdings, private-control blocks, government holdings, and legally restricted shares.

Note: International style indexes have received attention recently because plan sponsors have considered alternative structures for their international equity mandates, but none of the providers has a long-standing presence in this area. For example, MSCI only recently introduced style indexes (base date for MSCI value–growth indexes is December 31, 1996, with backfilled monthly data to December 31, 1974, for most developed markets). These value and growth indexes will each represent approximately half of the current index capitalization divided on the basis of price-to-book ratio. This approach is similar to the one used by S&P/BARRA in creating U.S. value and growth indexes but differs from the more sophisticated nonlinear probability methodology of Frank Russell Company and the screen-based approach of Wilshire Associates.

[a]MSCI recently introduced small-cap indexes (base date December 31, 1996, with back history calculated to December 31, 1992). These indexes aim to capture 40 percent of the small-cap universe (companies with $200 million to $800 million in market capitalization), so there is some overlap with the standard MSCI indexes.

[b]Whereas MSCI World Index and SSB BMI include the same 22 countries as of December 1996, the FT/S&P-AWI excludes four emerging markets (Brazil, Mexico, Thailand, and South Africa) because SSB and MSCI include them in their emerging market indexes.

[c]Return history begins December 31, 1980, but this history was back-filled using the December 1985 constituent list. As a result, considerable survivorship bias is associated with the data between December 1980 and December 1985.

Source: MSCI, Goldman Sachs, and Salomon Smith Barney.

Table 3.3. Benchmark Comparison among MSCI World Index Countries, December 1996

Country/Region	Index Market Cap ($ billions)			Companies in Index			Percent of Total Market Cap in Index		
	MSCI World	FT/S&P-AWI	SSB BMI	MSCI World	FT/S&P-AWI	SSB BMI	MSCI World	FT/S&P-AWI	SSB BMI
Austria	$23.8	$20.5	$15.1	24	24	33	65%	56%	41%
Belgium	67.9	90.5	54.7	17	27	38	59	79	47
Denmark	50.5	44.6	40.8	24	30	51	70	62	56
Finland	38.2	40.1	41.6	20	24	36	62	65	67
France	395.0	441.3	318.2	71	93	198	66	73	53
Germany	465.9	495.2	379.4	68	59	162	72	76	59
Ireland	19.6	25.3	25.7	11	16	30	58	75	76
Italy	175.6	170.1	114.5	55	58	87	70	67	45
Netherlands	269.8	290.6	287.6	22	19	82	69	74	73
Norway	31.5	30.6	29.0	24	35	44	54	53	50
Spain	129.0	145.5	98.5	31	35	55	67	75	51
Sweden	143.8	176.8	155.2	31	48	80	60	74	65
Switzerland	321.0	340.1	328.0	38	35	97	79	84	81
United Kingdom	1,093.6	1,382.9	1,369.3	137	212	583	63	79	79
Europe	$3,225.3	$3,694.2	$3,257.5	573	715	1,576	66	76	67
Australia	168.3	201.0	204.1	55	76	174	55	66	67
Hong Kong	214.6	299.3	219.0	38	59	138	55	76	56
Japan	1,842.4	2,386.9	1,655.5	309	480	1,550	60	78	54
Malaysia	148.3	148.8	125.3	76	107	254	48	48	41
New Zealand	22.9	24.5	18.0	10	14	20	60	64	47
Singapore[a]	76.7	66.7	56.8	37	43	90	52	46	39
Far East	$2,473.2	$3,127.3	$2,278.6	525	779	2,226	58	73	53
Canada	269.6	315.0	294.7	85	115	295	58	68	64
United States	4,549.1	5,926.2	5,982.5	379	623	2,998	58	76	76
North America	$4,818.7	$6,241.1	$6,277.2	464	738	3,293	58	75	76
Total	$10,517.2	$13,062.6	$11,813.3	1,562	2,232	7,095	60%	75%	68%

[a]MSCI also has a Singapore Free Index that reflects the fact that certain securities must trade on the foreign board once the foreign-ownership limit is reached. The methodology, however, is under revision because the Singapore Free Index market cap, which is supposed to reflect investability restrictions, is larger than that of the standard index as a result of shares trading at a premium on the foreign board. Note also that Malaysia was combined with Singapore prior to April 30, 1993.

Sources: MSCI, Goldman Sachs, and Salomon Smith Barney.

Table 3.4. Comparison among MSCI EAFE Countries, December 1996

	Market-Cap-Based Weights			Alternative Weights		
Country/Region	MSCI[a]	FT/S&P	SSB	MSCI GDP-Spot[b]	FT/S&P Cross-Holding Adjusted[c]	SSB GDP-PPP-Weighted[d]
Austria	0.4%	0.3%	0.3%	1.6%	0.4%	1.6%
Belgium	1.2	1.3	1.0	2.0	1.6	2.2
Denmark	0.9	0.7	0.7	1.4	0.8	1.4
Finland	0.7	0.6	0.8	1.2	0.7	1.1
France	6.9	6.5	5.7	11.6	7.8	11.5
Germany	8.2	7.3	6.9	20.2	8.7	15.6
Ireland	0.3	0.4	0.5	0.5	0.4	0.6
Italy	3.1	2.5	2.1	8.7	3.0	10.2
Netherlands	4.7	4.3	5.2	3.1	5.1	3.2
Norway	0.6	0.4	0.5	1.2	0.5	1.2
Spain	2.3	2.1	1.8	4.7	2.6	6.5
Sweden	2.5	2.6	2.8	2.0	3.1	1.9
Switzerland	5.6	5.0	5.9	2.1	6.0	1.5
United Kingdom	19.2	20.3	24.7	9.0	24.4	12.2
Europe	56.6%	54.2%	58.8%	69.1%	65.1%	70.7%
Australia	3.0	2.9	3.7	2.6	3.5	3.8
Hong Kong	3.8	4.4	4.0	1.1	5.3	1.7
Japan	32.3	35.0	29.9	25.6	21.9	20.6
Malaysia	2.6	2.2	2.3	0.6	2.6	1.8
New Zealand	0.4	0.4	0.3	0.4	0.4	0.7
Singapore	1.3	1.0	1.0	0.6	1.2	0.7
Far East	43.4%	45.8%	41.2%	30.9%	34.9%	29.3%
Canada	0	0	0	0	0	0
United States	0	0	0	0	0	0
North America	0	0	0	0	0	0
Total	100.0%	100.0%	100.0%	100.0%	100.0%	100.0%

[a]Portugal was added to the MSCI EAFE Index in December 1997.

[b]GDP is translated at year-end exchange rates.

[c]Only the Japan market capitalization is adjusted for cross-holdings. The Goldman Sachs approach in this index differs from the approach Salomon Smith Barney takes in the BMI, principally in terms of how bank cross-holdings are handled. Both benchmark providers rely on the Toyo Keizai, a Japanese economic and financial publishing company, which lists the 20 largest cross-holdings of a firm. Through its relationship with Frank Russell and Nomura Research Institute (or Russell/NRI), Goldman Sachs makes some additional adjustments based on annual reports and interviews with the banks.

[d]GDP is translated at purchasing power parity exchange rates.

Sources: MSCI, Goldman Sachs, and Salomon Smith Barney.

three countries are 8, 3, and 19 percent, respectively. The representation of the United Kingdom falls from the second largest in the market-cap-weighted index to the level of Italy in the GDP-weighted index. Because a large portion of Italian GDP is generated by state-owned enterprises that are unavailable to investors, holding a GDP weight in Italy requires "tripling up" on the purchasable equity issues. So, although an alternative index methodology may be attractive because it results in a comfortable policy weight in Japan, the price of that adjustment may be undesirable strategic statements in other countries.

The effect of these weighting schemes is illustrated in Figure 3.1. With the exception of the MSCI World Index and the FT/S&P-AWI, which track one another relatively closely, aggregate returns on an MSCI EAFE basket of countries can vary by several hundred basis points in a given year, which reflects differences not only in country exposures but also in currency, industry, and company exposures.

To conclude the discussion of international developed market indexes,

Figure 3.1. Comparison of Alternative Indexes, 1994–96
(based on December 1996 weights for an EAFE basket of countries)

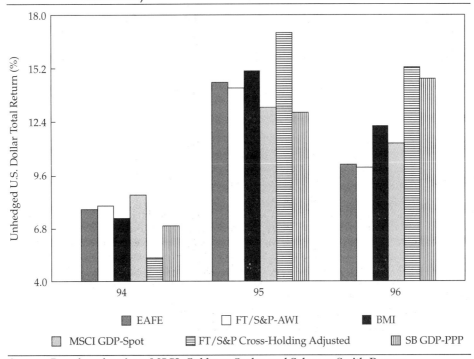

Sources: Based on data from MSCI, Goldman Sachs, and Salomon Smith Barney.

three additional observations concerning the MSCI EAFE Index merit mention. First, although most investors are aware that Japan carries a large weight in EAFE, as indicated in Table 3.4, the magnitude of the "Japan bet" is often underappreciated. As Figure 3.2 illustrates, using EAFE as the basis for gaining international equity exposure over the past two decades translated into roughly a 50 percent stake in Japan, a 20 percent position in the United Kingdom, and a 30 percent spread among 18 other countries.[5] Therefore, using EAFE as the basis for concluding that the volatility reduction provided by international equity has come at too steep a return cost is tantamount to concluding that the performance of a single country invalidates the case for international diversification.

The second observation also concerns the dominance of Japan in the MSCI EAFE Index, as illustrated in Figure 3.3. The Japanese representation in EAFE is basically the same in 1996 as in 1980, and active-manager perfor-

Figure 3.2. MSCI EAFE Index Return Disaggregation, January 1978–December 1996

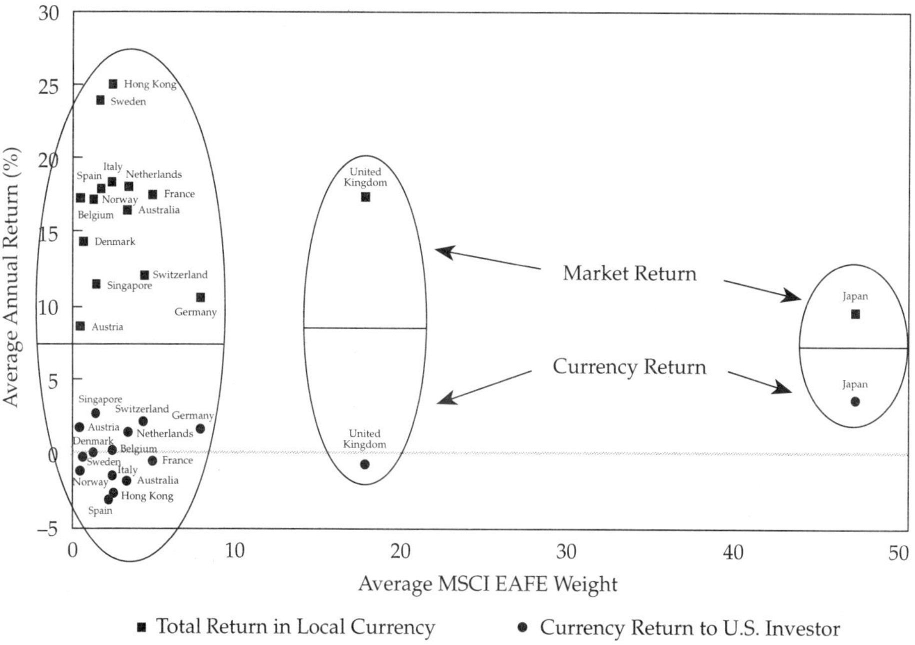

Source: Based on data from MSCI.

---

[5]Actually, the total number of countries was 14 until New Zealand and Finland were added to the MSCI EAFE Index on December 31, 1987, and the total was 16 until Ireland and Malaysia were added on April 30, 1993.

46

Figure 3.3. Japan and Active-Manager Performance, January 1980–December 1996
(trailing 12-month data)

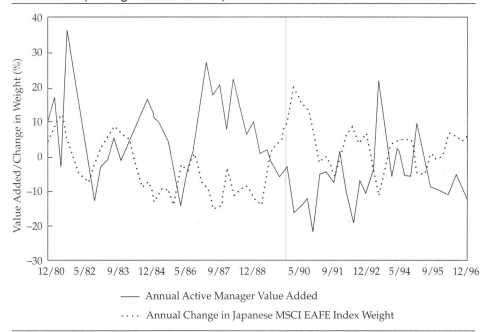

    ——— Annual Active Manager Value Added
    · · · · Annual Change in Japanese MSCI EAFE Index Weight

Source: Based on data from the WM Company and MSCI.

mance during those 17 years was basically flat relative to the index. These unremarkable statistics conceal a very dichotomous sample period, however. During the 1990s, active managers' annual average alpha was –2.8 percent and the annual average change in the Japanese weight in EAFE was 6.7 percent. During the 1980s, the annual averages were 3.2 percent and –8.2 percent, respectively. Because active managers regularly underweighted Japan relative to EAFE during this period as a result of concerns about cross-holdings or P/E multiples, they tended to underperform the index when the EAFE weight in Japan increased.[6] Such was the case during the 1980s, when active managers trailed the index by almost 300 basis points (bps) a year. During the 1990s, the opposite occurred. Active managers outperformed the index by more than 300 bps a year as the significance of Japan in EAFE diminished.

---

[6]Obviously, a rise in the EAFE weight in Japan indicates Japanese outperformance of the EAFE Index, excluding Japan. This result can be interpreted *loosely* as Japanese outperformance of the alternative markets available to active managers.

For the period from January 1980 to December 1996, the correlation between value added by active managers and the change in the Japanese EAFE weight was approximately –0.60.

Third, the influence of the largest companies on the country indexes that compose the MSCI EAFE Index varies widely. As Figure 3.4 illustrates, the five largest companies account for only 18 percent of the Japan Index capitalization, but five firms account for more than 70 percent of the index performance in Finland and the Netherlands. One must be careful in assessing the diversification benefits of countries whose performance is so dependent on the fortunes of only a handful of companies.

Emerging Market Indexes

In emerging market benchmarks, two principal providers of return data—MSCI and the International Finance Corporation (IFC)—offer two classes of emerging market benchmarks: global (or unadjusted), and investable (or

Figure 3.4. Five Largest Companies as a Share of MSCI EAFE Index Capitalization in Developed Markets, December 1996

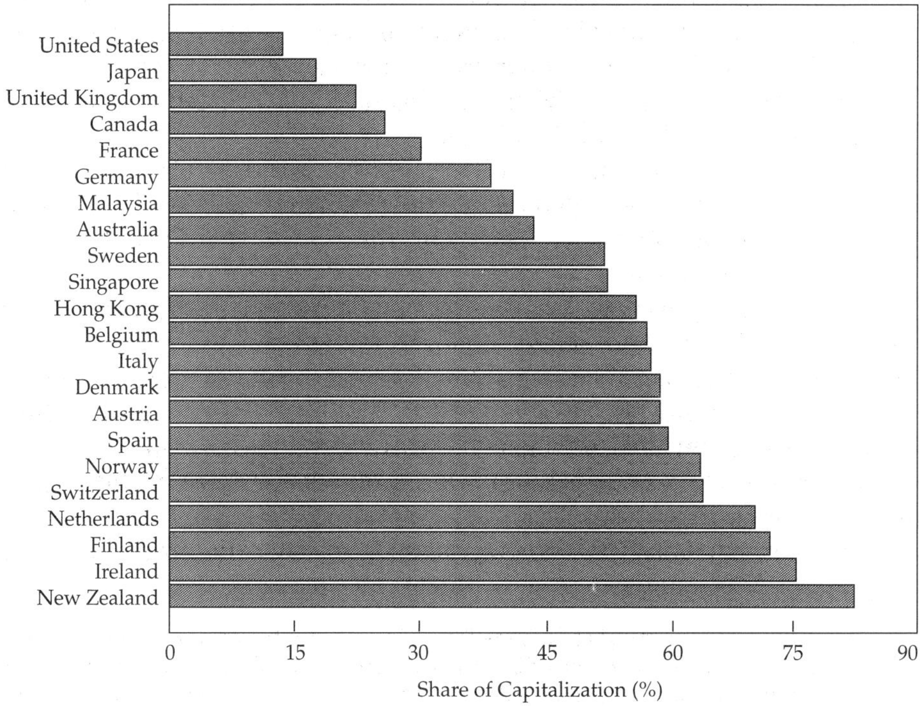

Source: Based on data from MSCI and FactSet.

free).[7] The IFC, a member of the World Bank Group, has the longer tradition of compiling data on emerging market equity, but neither data provider has established a dominant position among U.S. plan sponsors.

The principal difference between the two data providers, beyond slightly broader market coverage by the IFC, is the manner in which they handle investability, as indicated in Table 3.5 and Table 3.6. The IFC makes the more concerted effort to reflect the numerous restrictions that foreign investors encounter when attempting to purchase emerging market stocks. As a result, the IFC Investable Composite Index serves as the basis for emerging market analysis in this monograph. This benchmark has three notable characteristics:

- As of December 1996, investability adjustments reduce the index market capitalization by 35 percent. These changes have the greatest impact on the Asia/Far East representation because of the exclusion of more than half the capitalization surviving the initial IFC screens in Korea, India, China, Philippines, Taiwan, and Thailand. As a result, the 61 percent global weight in this region is reduced to a 46 percent investable weight, as shown in Table 3.7.
- Five countries—Malaysia, South Africa, Brazil, Mexico, and Taiwan (in order of IFC Investable weight as of December 1996)—account for approximately two-thirds of the index market capitalization. This total is less than the almost three-quarters of index capitalization represented by the five largest countries (France, Germany, Japan, United Kingdom, and Switzerland) in the MSCI EAFE Index.
- Despite the methodological differences that lead to discrepancies in country weights, the regional exposures in the IFC and MSCI indexes to Latin America, Asia/Far East, and Europe/Middle East/Africa are actually very similar.

The emerging markets, like the developed international markets, have lagged the United States significantly from 1992 to 1996. Table 3.8 presents the historical performance of the various emerging market indexes relative to that of the United States. The average return of the emerging markets from 1994 to 1996 was negative, principally because of poor performance in Mexico and Thailand. Table 3.8 also highlights the magnitude of the return differences among the indexes.

Diversifying among the emerging markets is crucial (in particular, to take

---

[7]ING Barings offers the Emerging Markets World Index (BEMI), which is liquidity oriented with a large-cap bias, and the Emerging Markets Extended World Index, which is less concentrated. The BEMI was introduced in October 1992 and has a reconstructed return history back to December 1987. Because U.S. plan sponsors typically use the IFC or MSCI benchmark, the BEMI is excluded from the summary tables.

Table 3.5 Emerging Market Equity Benchmark Methodology Comparison

Index	Length of Return History	Breadth of Coverage	Adjustments to Market-Cap Weighting[a]
MSCI Emerging Markets	Inception: 12/31/87	60 percent of total market cap for all industries	MSCI considers liquidity, free float, and cross-holdings in selecting securities. Once selected, securities are typically included at full market cap (both listed and unlisted shares included).
IFC Global Composite	Inception: 12/31/84[b]	60–75 percent of total market cap for all industries	The IFC focuses on including only the most actively traded securities.
MSCI Emerging Markets Free	Inception: 12/31/87		MSCI adjusts market cap to reflect foreign-ownership restrictions on certain classes of shares in Mexico and the Philippines. MSCI also reduces the weighting of Taiwan and Korea by 50 percent.
IFC Investable Composite	Inception: 2/28/93[c]		The IFC adjusts market cap to reflect cross-holdings and legal restrictions, such as special classes of shares, sector restrictions, single-foreign-shareholder limits, and national limits on aggregate foreign investment. The IFC then includes securities having an adjusted market cap of $25 million or more (exceptions are made for heavily traded securities) and an annual value traded of at least $10 million.

Note: The benchmarks are composed principally of middle-income economies (i.e., $766–$9,385 per capita gross national product in 1995), although some low-income (e.g., India) and high-income (e.g., Israel) economies are included.
[a]Although these indexes are all capitalization weighted, equal-weighted variants are used occasionally.
[b]Some country-level return histories back-filled to December 31, 1975, which introduces survivorship bias.
[c]Return history reconstructed to December 31, 1988.
Sources: MSCI and IFC.

Table 3.6. Benchmark Comparisons among Emerging Markets, December 1996

Country/Region[a]	Index Market Cap ($ billions)			Companies in Index			Percent of Total Market Cap in Index		
	MSCI EMG[b]	IFCG[c]	IFCI[d]	MSCI EMG	IFCG	IFCI	MSCI EMG	IFCG	IFCI
Argentina	$30.6	$26.6	$26.4	23	35	31	69%	59%	59%
Brazil	109.9	94.9	77.4	61	86	68	51	44	36
Chile	31.8	35.8	35.5	32	47	45	48	54	54
Colombia	5.8	9.3	7.1	9	27	14	34	54	41
Mexico	74.6	72.2	66.8	44	76	64	70	68	63
Peru	8.6	7.6	7.1	14	36	19	62	55	51
Venezuela	9.8	7.2	6.3	14	18	9	97	71	63
Latin America	$271.1	$253.5	$226.6	197	325	250	57%	53%	48%
China	5.1	38.8	4.8	26	180	27	4	34	4
India	48.0	50.8	13.0	67	131	79	39	41	11
Indonesia	48.9	49.6	30.8	39	50	49	54	55	34
Korea	77.3	73.1	16.1	116	162	156	56	53	12
Malaysia	148.3	169.9	156.2	76	148	148	48	55	51
Pakistan	5.4	4.6	3.7	33	64	28	51	44	35
Philippines	36.3	48.6	22.3	35	52	42	45	60	28
Sri Lanka	0.6	1.1	0.4	10	47	5	33	61	19
Taiwan	158.8	151.4	49.6	77	90	90	58	55	18
Thailand	42.7	57.7	19.7	76	88	87	43	58	20
Asia/Far East	$571.4	$645.8	$316.6	555	1,012	711	37%	52%	26%
Czech Republic	11.3	9.6	3.4	20	74	7	62	53	19
Greece	10.3	10.2	10.1	36	58	54	43	42	42
Hungary	3.5	3.6	3.2	9	18	12	67	68	61
Israel	18.3	0	0	50	0	0	51	0	0
Jordan	1.1	2.9	0.8	15	51	7	25	63	17
Poland	4.3	5.7	5.7	18	31	30	51	69	17
Portugal	17.5	16.4	12.7	23	32	28	71	67	51
Nigeria	0	2.5	0	0	35	0	0	70	0
South Africa	97.0	86.1	86.1	56	63	63	40	36	36
Turkey	12.3	16.3	16.3	45	58	58	41	54	54
Zimbabwe	0	2.4	0.6	0	22	5	0	66	17
Europe/Middle East/Africa	$175.6	$155.7	$138.8	272	442	264	44%	39%	35%
Composite	$1,018.2	$1,054.9	$682.0	1,024	1,779	1,225	48%	50%	32%

Note: MSCI EMG = Emerging Markets Global Index, IFCG = IFC Global Index, IFCI = IFC Investable Composite Index.

[a]MSCI and the IFC cover additional countries that had not been added to their respective composite benchmarks as of December 1996.

[b]The MSCI Emerging Markets Free Index differs from the EMG Index in two ways: (1) MSCI calculates Mexico Free ($71.9 billion, 41 countries) and Philippines Free ($30.4 billion, 30 countries) indexes, and (2) MSCI half-weights Korea ($38.7 billion) and Taiwan ($79.4 billion). MSCI uses the same China Free Index in the global and investable composites. Also, note that MSCI will add Russia to the EMG in December 1997.

[c]The IFC added Egypt, Morocco, and Russia to the IFCG Index in January 1997. Israel and Slovakia were added in November 1997.

[d]The IFC added Egypt, Morocco, Russia, Israel, and Slovakia to the Investable Composite Index in November 1997.

Sources: MSCI and the IFC.

Table 3.7. Emerging Market Country-Weight Comparisons, December 1996

Country/Region	Global Index		Investable Index	
	MSCI	IFC	MSCI	IFC
Argentina	3.0%	2.5%	3.4%	3.9%
Brazil	10.8	9.0	12.3	11.3
Chile	3.1	3.4	3.6	5.2
Colombia	0.6	0.9	0.6	1.0
Mexico	7.3	6.8	8.1	9.8
Peru	0.8	0.7	1.0	1.0
Venezuela	1.0	0.7	1.1	0.9
Latin America	26.6%	24.0%	30.1%	33.2%
China[a]	0.5	3.7	0.6	0.7
India	4.7	4.8	5.4	1.9
Indonesia	4.8	4.7	5.5	4.5
Korea	7.6	6.9	4.3	2.4
Malaysia	14.6	16.1	16.6	22.9
Pakistan	0.5	0.4	0.6	0.5
Philippines	3.6	4.6	3.4	3.3
Sri Lanka	0.1	0.1	0.1	0.1
Taiwan	15.6	14.4	8.9	7.3
Thailand	4.2	5.5	4.8	2.9
Asia/Far East	56.1%	61.2%	50.2%	46.4%
Czech Republic	1.1	0.9	1.3	0.5
Greece	1.0	1.0	1.2	1.5
Hungary	0.3	0.3	0.4	0.5
Israel	1.8	0	2.1	0
Jordan	0.1	0.3	0.1	0.1
Poland	0.4	0.5	0.5	0.8
Portugal	1.7	1.6	2.0	1.9
Nigeria	0	0.2	0	0
South Africa	9.5	8.2	10.9	12.6
Turkey	1.2	1.5	1.4	2.4
Zimbabwe	0	0.2	0	0.1
Europe/Middle East/Africa	17.2%	14.8%	19.7%	20.4%
Total	100.0%	100.0%	100.0%	100.0%

[a]The Chinese index (Global and Investable) includes H-shares (listings on the Hong Kong Stock Exchange in Hong Kong dollars), B-shares (domestic listings on the Shanghai and Shenzhen exchanges that are available to foreign investors), and N-shares (listings on the New York Stock Exchange in U.S. dollars). The IFC Global Index also includes A-shares (domestic listings that are available only to local investors). "Red chip" stocks, which are Hong Kong holding companies for mainland Chinese assets, account for a significant percentage of available Chinese capitalization but are not included in any MSCI or IFC indexes (China or Hong Kong) because of their ambiguous lineage. (For reference, the Hang Seng Red Chip Index is composed of 36 such companies.)

Sources: MSCI and IFC.

Table 3.8. Emerging Market Annualized Performance Summary

Period/Measurement	Global		Investable		
	IFC	MSCI	IFC	MSCI	United States
Past eight years (1989–96)[a]					
Average return	11.3%	13.4%	19.6%	22.7%	13.1%
Standard deviation	22.1	23.0	23.7	26.4	17.0
Past five years (1992–96)					
Average return	11.1	12.5	12.2	14.3	16.8
Standard deviation	18.6	19.2	20.9	19.9	16.8
Past three years (1994–96)					
Average return	–0.9	–0.5	–2.6	–1.1	16.0
Standard deviation	15.0	14.9	17.3	16.0	9.9

[a]Unhedged into U.S. dollars.
[b]Earliest available data for IFC Investable Composite Index.
Sources: The IFC and MSCI.

advantage of the low correlations among the three emerging market regions—Latin America, Asia/Far East, and Europe/Middle East/Africa). Figure 3.5 illustrates the degree to which return volatility in the individual emerging markets differs from that in the United States. The need for diversification in emerging markets is demonstrated by the observation that the index-level volatility for the IFC Investable Composite over this period was only 17 percent but that Brazil, one of the largest constituents of the index, had an annual return volatility in excess of 50 percent.

A three-year time period was selected in Figure 3.5 in order to present a standard deviation of returns for each of the 26 countries currently included in the IFC Investable Composite Index. Obviously, the miserable returns reflect a few significant events, such as the collapse of the Mexican peso in late 1994 and the recent woes in Thailand. The paucity of historical data concerning emerging markets is common knowledge, and only 10 of those 26 countries were included in the IFC Investable Composite eight years before. As recently as 1992, the index did not include two of the five largest current constituents (South Africa and Taiwan, which currently constitute 20 percent of the index).

The degree to which a few large companies drive country-level returns is also an important consideration. As shown in Figure 3.6, some of the smaller markets are dominated by several companies, but such market dominance is not true across the board. In fact, contrary to the common perception that returns in most emerging markets are driven by the fortunes of a few companies, the cap-weighted role of the five largest firms among the emerging markets in Figure 3.6 is actually *lower* than that among the developed markets

Figure 3.5. Emerging Market Equity Risk–Return Profile, January 1994–December 1996

(three-year unhedged returns)

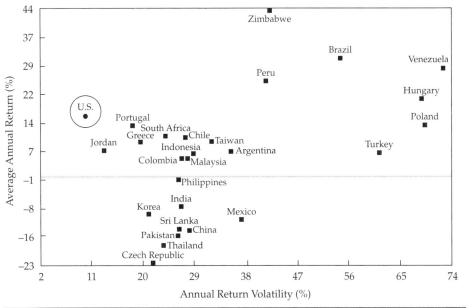

Note: Scale for annual return appears irregular because of rounding.

Source: Based on data from the IFC.

(excluding the United States and Japan) shown in Figure 3.4.

Summary

Like it or not, past returns play an important role in the generation of the return, volatility, and correlation expectations that drive strategic asset allocations. The information on international return indexes provided in this chapter is intended to help plan sponsors guard against the introduction of unwanted biases in the forecasting process. After all, an informed consumer of historical data is a better decision maker.

Figure 3.6. Five Largest Companies as a Share of IFC Investable Emerging Market Capitalization, December 1996

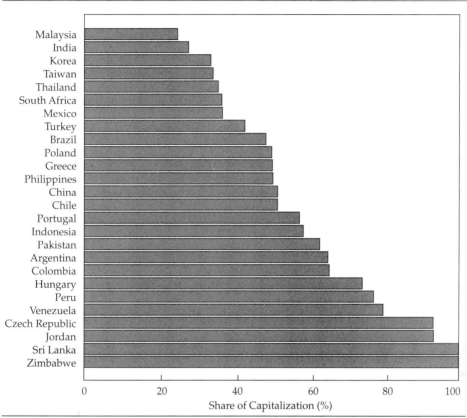

Source: Based on data from IFC and FactSet.

4. Key Fundamentals: Currency, Correlations, and Costs

The fundamental issues of currency, correlations, and costs are pivotal considerations in any decision about international equity. For currency, this chapter develops the case for a 50 percent hedge ratio by assessing the economic theory of international parity and how it relates to the arguments for the three basic approaches to policy-level exchange rate management—zero hedging, full hedging, and partial hedging. In regard to correlations, the analysis focuses on the fashionable trend of equating increasing global integration with rising correlations and demonstrates why such a conclusion is a gross oversimplification. The discussion concludes with a detailed investigation of the costs associated with international equity.

Currency

U.S. investors experienced 10 distinct periods of currency returns in the two decades ending December 1996—five of U.S. dollar weakness and five of dollar strength—as indicated by Table 4.1. These periods varied in length between approximately one year and four years and tested the resolve of those assuming currency returns to be insignificant in the long term. Weak- and strong-dollar regimes resulted in average annual currency returns of 17 percent and –10 percent, respectively.

Although Morgan Stanley Capital International (MSCI) EAFE (Europe/Australasia/Far East) Index currency returns were heavily influenced by the Japanese yen, the results in Table 4.1 are robust to any of the alternative index weighting schemes discussed in Chapter 3. Figure 4.1 depicts very consistent changes in the major exchange rates. During a strong-dollar regime, being long the dollar was far more important than owning the right foreign currency. Likewise, during a weak-dollar regime, being unhedged was generally more important than the actual currency exposure selected. These points may appear to be trivial, but the amount of protection provided by a diversified basket of currencies is often overstated. Although exchange rates certainly do not change in a lockstep fashion, the correlation of yen returns, for example, with those of most major currencies exceeded 0.6 over this period. As indicated by the high average correlations in Figure 4.1, the correlation among the returns on many European currencies surpassed 0.9 during this time.

Table 4.1. Currency Performance Disaggregation, December 1977–December 1996

Period	Duration (months)	Annualized Currency Return
12/77–10/78	10	29.7%
10/78–3/80	17	−11.1
3/80–12/80	9	15.0
12/80–2/85	50	−10.3
2/85–12/87	34	27.3
12/87–8/89	20	−9.4
8/89–8/92	36	7.4
8/92–12/93	16	−5.9
12/93–6/95	18	14.5
6/95–12/96	18	−8.5

Note: Shaded row = dollar weakness; unshaded row = dollar strength.
Source: MSCI.

Based on which currency index?.

In summary, employing unhedged benchmarks under the assumption that a diversified currency basket will limit currency losses is an ill-advised strategy. Two factors undermine this approach. First, currency return correlations are high and, therefore, do little to reduce portfolio volatility. (A correlation simply describes the path to an average return but indicates nothing about the average return itself.) Second, although highly correlated assets can generate very different average returns, such is not the case with currencies. There is a directional uniformity to average currency returns—negative returns come in bunches. As a result, a diversified portfolio of the major currencies simply does not provide much protection, particularly over a single strategic planning period.

Note that this analysis does not apply to the emerging markets. As Table 4.2 indicates, some developing countries' problems (such as chronic budget deficits, lax monetary policies, or balance-of-payments crises) have translated into very negative currency returns for U.S. investors regardless of the dollar regime. In emerging markets, however, negative currency returns can have a positive side. Obviously, the negative translation effect presented in Table 4.2 is a drag on the total return realized by foreign investors, but negative currency returns may reflect appropriate policy decisions (e.g., austerity measures with respect to government spending). Necessary currency devaluation can produce substantial equity market gains, as was the case in Argentina in 1991 and Brazil in 1994. The dramatic nature and pace of changes occurring in emerging markets make this effect more significant than in the developed markets. Of course, inappropriate policies that undermine the currency can have dire consequences in the equity market (e.g., Mexico in late 1994).

Figure 4.1. Global Currency Returns, January 1978–December 1996

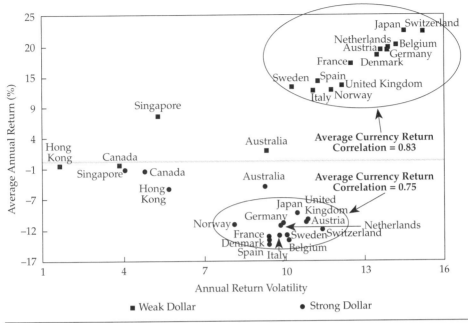

Note: Return scale appears irregular because of rounding.
Source: Based on data from MSCI and Ibbotson Associates.

Managers of emerging market portfolios generally deal with currency risk by liquidating equity holdings in markets associated with vulnerable currencies and by accepting the exchange rate exposure accompanying positions in attractive equity markets, often assuming that a strong economy will be good news for both the stock and currency markets. As Figure 4.2 and Exhibit 4.1 illustrate, forward markets do exist for many emerging market currencies, but wide short-term interest rate differentials (which make hedging prohibitively expensive) and/or low liquidity (particularly when it is needed most) currently prevent extensive currency hedging from being a realistic alternative in emerging market portfolios. For example, two years ago, the foreign exchange markets in Malaysia, Indonesia, and Thailand were reasonably liquid, each having an average daily turnover in excess of $1 billion. The 1997 collapse of the managed-float regimes in these countries has changed the situation. Interest rate differentials have widened, spreads on forward contracts have increased, and liquidity has evaporated—all of which make hedging considerably more difficult than was the case only two years ago. Recovery in these markets will take time.

Table 4.2. Developed versus Emerging Market Currency Performance

Period	Duration (months)	MSCI EAFE Annualized Currency Return	IFC Investable Annualized Currency Return
8/89–8/92	36	7.4%	–19.9%
8/92–12/93	16	–5.9	–30.6
12/93–6/95	18	14.5	–20.1
6/95–12/96	18	–8.5	–8.9

Source: MSCI and the International Finance Corporation.

Exchange Rate Exposure. Defining the proper strategic exchange rate exposure is among the more contentious issues pertaining to international diversification because of the duration of the dollar cycles and the magnitude of the accompanying currency returns. Investors debate three basic approaches to exchange rate management—zero hedging, full hedging, and partial hedging.

The first step in choosing an approach is to consider the economic theory that is typically invoked when discussing hedging policy. The theory of international parity depends on four interrelated equilibrium conditions: relative purchasing power parity, covered interest rate parity, the international Fisher relation, and uncovered interest rate parity.[1]

The key observation of relative purchasing power parity (PPP) is that exchange rate risk reduces to inflation uncertainty. If real exchange rates experience no fluctuation, the real return on an asset is equal regardless of the investor's base currency. Because, in reality, significant and persistent variation in real exchange rates does occur, relative PPP must assume *long-term* mean reversion in real exchange rates. The mathematical expression of relative PPP is

$$\Delta S = \frac{1 + I_F}{1 + I_D} - 1,$$

or $\Delta S \cong I_F - I_D$ in approximate form, where

ΔS = change in spot exchange rate[2]

I_F = inflation rate of the foreign country

I_D = inflation rate of the domestic country

Covered interest rate parity must hold in order to prevent riskless arbitrage. The equation is

---

[1]For a more thorough discussion of international parity relations, see Solnik (1996).

[2]Exchange rate quoted in foreign currency per unit of *numeraire* currency (e.g., for U.S. investor: yen per U.S. dollar).

©The Research Foundation of the ICFA

$$f = \frac{1 + r_F}{1 + r_D} - 1,$$

or the approximation $f \cong r_F - r_D$, where

f = forward discount/premium

r_F = nominal foreign interest rate

r_D = nominal domestic interest rate

Thus, the forward premium often referred to as the cost of hedging, is approximately equal to the interest rate differential between two countries.

The international Fisher relation holds that nominal interest rate differ-

Figure 4.2. Characteristics of the Currencies in the MSCI All Country World Index

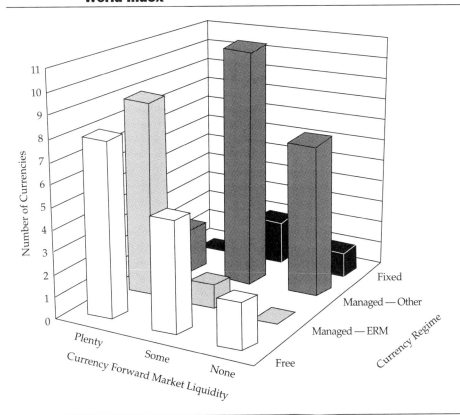

Note: "Managed—ERM" regime represents the currencies of the first-round EMU (European Monetary Union) entrants that all abide by the 15 percent fluctuation margin of the exchange rate mechanism of the European Monetary System. The "managed" regime is quite diverse, varying from informal pegs to relatively free float regimes.

Source: Based on data from Goldman, Sachs & Company and Lehman Brothers.

Exhibit 4.1. Currency Liquidity Summary, Third Quarter 1997[a]

Plenty	Some	None
Australian dollar	Argentinean peso	Chinese yuan renminbi
Austrian schilling	Brazilian real	Colombian peso
Belgian franc	Chilean peso	Indian rupee
Canadian dollar	Czech Republic koruna	Indonesian rupiah
Danish krone	Greek drachma	Israeli shekel
Finnish markka	Hong Kong dollar	Jordanian dinar
French franc	Hungarian forint	Pakistani rupee
German mark	Irish punt	Peruvian sol
Italian lira	Korean won	Philippine peso
Japanese yen	Malaysian ringgit	Sri Lankan rupee
Netherlands guilder	Mexican peso	
New Zealand dollar	Polish zloty	
Norwegian krone	Russian ruble	
Portuguese escudo	Singaporean dollar	
Spanish peseta	South African rand	
Swedish krona	Taiwanese dollar	
Swiss franc	Thai baht	
U.K. pound sterling	Turkish lira	
U.S. dollar	Venezuelan bolivar	

Note: Liquidity defined relative to index weight.

[a] A few currencies dominate the foreign exchange market. Specifically, 83 percent of global transactions involve the U.S. dollar; 37 percent, the German mark; and 24 percent, the Japanese yen. For details, see the "67th Annual Report, Bank for International Settlements, Fiscal Year April 1, 1996–March 31, 1997," submitted June 9, 1997 in Basel, Switzerland.

Sources: Goldman Sachs and Lehman Brothers.

ences reduce to inflation rate differences and that real interest rates are equal around the world. In actuality, real interest rates differ considerably among markets for lengthy periods of time. The international Fisher relation must, therefore, assume *long-term* mean reversion in real interest rates. The mathematical representation of for this relation is

$$\frac{1 + r_F}{1 + r_D} = \frac{1 + E[I_F]}{1 + E[I_D]},$$

or $r_F - r_D \cong E[I_F] - E[I_D]$, where $E[I_F]$ is the expected foreign inflation rate and $E[I_D]$ is the expected domestic inflation rate.

The basic tenet of uncovered interest rate parity is that relative to an unhedged position, eliminating currency risk has no expected-return implication. Investors thus get no reward for bearing exchange rate uncertainty (i.e., no risk premium). Because short-term departures from PPP and the international Fisher relation do occur, **uncovered interest rate parity must imply long-term mean reversion in the currency surprise** (i.e., the difference between the spot-rate change and the forward discount/premium) because forward exchange markets are not continually surprised in the same direction. The equation for uncovered interest rate parity is $E[\Delta S] = f$. (Some rewrite the equation to include a time-varying currency risk premium [RP] with a long-term average value of zero: $E[(S] = f + RP$.)

Figure 4.3 summarizes the links among the four relationships. Relative purchasing power parity connects spot exchange rate changes and inflation differentials. The International Fisher Relation connects inflation differentials and nominal interest rate differences. Covered interest rate parity connects nominal interest rate differences and forward premiums/discounts. Finally, uncovered interest rate parity connects forward premiums/discounts and spot exchange rate changes. In the interrelated system depicted in Figure 4.3, if purchasing power parity and the international Fisher relation hold, uncovered interest rate parity must hold so that forward premium/discounts reduce to

Figure 4.3. International Parity Relations

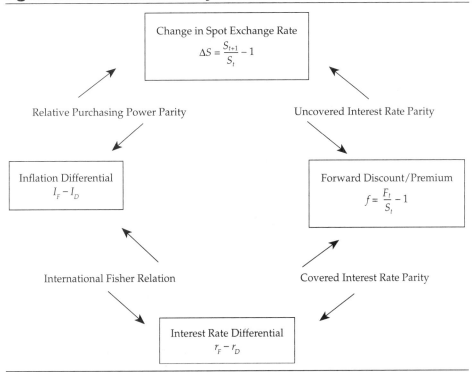

Note: Terms defined in previous parity equations.
Source: Based on an exhibit in Solnik (1996).

inflation differences and currency surprises are all zero.

A consensus view on hedging has not emerged because of the theory's unreliability over a single strategic planning period and the plausibility of the arguments for each of the three approaches to strategic currency management. Understanding the relationship between each of the four parity relations, as summarized in Figure 4.3, helps one to assess the efficacy of each of the three approaches to strategic currency management (i.e., zero hedging, full hedging, and partial hedging).

Zero hedging. This is a common choice among U.S. plan sponsors, who generally base their decision on some combination of the following four rationales. First, foreign currency exposure hedges a U.S. portfolio against inflationary monetary or fiscal policy in this country (i.e., against detrimental actions by the U.S. government or the Federal Reserve). For example, loose monetary policy ultimately pushes interest rates higher, which has an adverse effect on bond and stock returns. The dollar, however, tends to weaken in such an inflationary environment, so a U.S. investor realizes positive currency returns on unhedged international assets. Alternatively, this hedge can be viewed from a PPP perspective, in which the cost of both imports (weaker dollar) and domestic products (inflationary policy) rises but currency gains on unhedged overseas investments are available to offset the higher prices.

Another theory used to support zero hedging is that currency returns are irrelevant in the long run. On the return side, exchange rate fluctuations have no real return implication (i.e., PPP). Put another way, inflation in a given market should increase the local return, thereby offsetting the currency loss and ensuring that investors in all countries realize an equal real return. On the risk side, exchange rate exposure among many markets dampens aggregate currency return volatility, and negative correlations between currency and equity returns reduce further the impact of exchange rate fluctuations at the portfolio level. Consequently, strategic hedging is pointless, because the long-term real return on a broadly diversified basket of currencies should be zero, and the contribution of this basket to portfolio risk should be trivial.

A third argument in favor of zero hedging is that to the extent that U.S. pension liabilities are denominated in other currencies, a plan should protect itself by including similar exchange rate exposures in its portfolio.

Finally, given that most U.S. plans have only small international positions, the marginal benefit of even a prescient hedging policy is minimal after one considers the expense and logistical headaches. Consider the three primary effects of hedging: It reduces the return volatility of international assets, increases the correlation of international assets with U.S. assets, and reduces the correlation among international assets. If the stake in non-U.S. assets is small, the portfolio will not benefit enough from the first and third risk-reduction effects so as to offset the second effect and any hedging-related costs.

▩ *Full hedging.* Full hedging is an unpopular choice among U.S. plan sponsors. Those in favor of this approach emphasize that, in the long term, currency hedging is a zero-expected-return undertaking (i.e., the long-run reward for bearing currency risk will not be one sided; any currency risk premium will be transitory and unstable in terms of sign and magnitude).[3] The linkages in Figure 4.3 indicate that, over time, unhedged returns should equal hedged returns, because both interest rate differentials and exchange rate changes reduce to inflation differentials. If no long-term benefit is associated with exchange rate uncertainty, this risk should be avoided. In short, because hedging provides substantial risk reduction *in real terms*, can be accomplished at no expected return loss, and is not prohibitively costly, international assets should be fully hedged in the strategic portfolio.

▩ *Partial hedging.* More popular than full hedging among U.S. plan sponsors but less popular than zero hedging, partial hedging is supported by those who believe that a middle ground exists between the two hedging policy extremes.[4] The ICAPM model of Solnik (1974a) is the best known example. In equilibrium, investors of all nations hold a combination of the risk-free asset (which in the presence of exchange rate uncertainty is the domestic T-bill) and the global market portfolio hedged in the same way against currency risk. The optimal hedge ratio can differ by asset, so the hedge ratio of the foreign portfolio depends on the domicile of the investor. Black (1989) proposed a generalized version of this model requiring only three inputs that has a single, universal hedge ratio. In other words, given that everyone holds the global market portfolio, investors of all countries should hedge an identical proportion of each asset.[5]

One analysis of real returns provides another basis for partial hedging. Froot (1993) demonstrated that hedge returns are driven by real exchange rate variation in the short term (i.e., less than three years), which makes

---

[3]See Perold and Schulman (1988).

[4]Some plan sponsors who assign unhedged benchmarks but permit active, defensive hedging regard themselves as partially hedged strategically. This group is classified as having a zero hedging policy in this monograph.

[5]See Black (1989). The optimal hedge ratio is $\dfrac{\mu_M - \sigma_M^2}{\mu_M - 0.5\sigma_E^2}$, where μ_M is the average risk premium on the market portfolio and σ_M and σ_E are the average market portfolio and exchange rate volatility, respectively. This equation provides only the aggregate proportion to hedge. It provides no information on the hedge composition.

hedging a risk-*reducing* activity relative to an unhedged benchmark. In the long term, however, hedge returns are dominated by intercountry differences in real interest rates and unexpected inflation, which render hedging a risk-*enhancing* activity relative to an unhedged benchmark. Because plan sponsors are concerned with both horizons, the work by Froot suggests a policy of partial hedging.

Other proponents of partial hedging emphasize the many inconsistencies between theory and reality that make exclusive reliance on theory a worrisome proposition. For example, they hold that transaction costs and trade barriers restrict arbitrage and that different consumption preferences and baskets hinder inflation comparisons. One approach favored by some in this group endorses a systematic bet against uncovered interest rate parity. Because the direction of interest rate differentials tends to change gradually and assuming the current spot rate is a better predictor of the future exchange rate than is the forward rate, this approach supports completely hedging only those currencies for which the forward exchange rate is at a premium (i.e., when one is paid to hedge).[6] The aggregate portfolio hedge ratio is thus a function of the preponderance of premium currencies relative to the U.S. dollar.

Of the three approaches to hedging, the two extremes—zero and full hedging—suffer from the practical limitation of reliance on some nebulous "long run." Given the three- to five-year planning horizon of most plan sponsors, frequent significant and protracted deviations from equilibrium exchange rates (as indicated by Table 4.1) and the lack of academic consensus on hedging policy, prudence dictates using a 50 percent hedge ratio as the strategic base case. Departures from this "prior" may be made as conditions warrant. For example, an interest rate environment in which hedging is extremely expensive (i.e., most major currencies are at a discount relative to the U.S. dollar) might necessitate a somewhat lower ratio. Alternatively, indications from a long-run fundamental currency model that the dollar is very cheap against some of the major currencies could prompt a slightly higher hedge ratio. The bottom line is that careful consideration must be given to an appropriate hedge ratio and that the proper amount of currency exposure is somewhere between zero and 100 percent.

Some practical justification for the partial hedging approach is provided in Figure 4.4, which shows the mid-1997 forward premiums/discounts of the MSCI World Index currencies relative to the U.S. dollar. Because of relatively high interest rates in the United States, a significant number of premium currencies relative to the dollar are available, and as a result, a U.S. investor

---

[6]See Eaker and Grant (1990).

Figure 4.4. Expected Annual Currency Returns to a U.S.-Based Investor, Second Quarter 1997

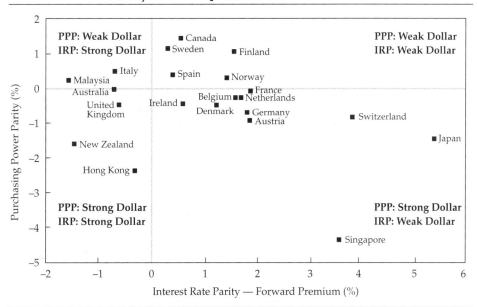

is paid to hedge. The dollar is the discount currency and, therefore, is expected to *weaken* in 15 of 21 instances. (A weakening dollar translates into positive currency returns for an unhedged U.S. investor, whereas a strengthening dollar results in currency losses.) In Japan, for example, U.S. investors are paid more than 500 basis points (bps) a year to hedge. This guaranteed payment represents a substantial hurdle to clear with an imprecise yen return forecast on unhedged Japanese assets.

The vertical axis of Figure 4.4 represents expected currency returns to an unhedged investor as proxied by PPP. By this measure, the dollar is under-valued and is expected to *strengthen* versus 14 of 21 currencies, including all of the major ones. The inconsistent direction currently provided by interest rate parity and PPP is yet another justification for the "neutral" positioning provided by a 50 percent hedge ratio.

One additional point warrants mention with respect to partial hedging. The role of hedging in reducing equity portfolio volatility is small given the current international exposure of most U.S. pension plans, as illustrated by Figure 4.5.[7] Only at significant international equity allocations does hedg-

---

[7]Note, however, that if the often lamented 20–25 bp cost of a hedging program is assessed in the same total portfolio context, it becomes inconsequential, too.

Figure 4.5. Effect of Hedging on Portfolio Volatility, January 1978–December 1996

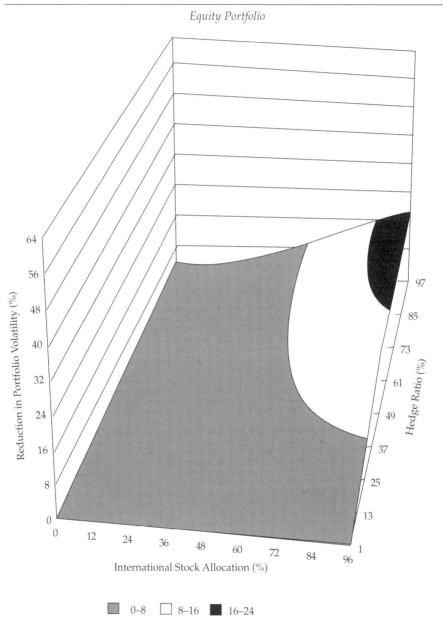

Equity Portfolio

Source: Based on data from MSCI and Salomon Smith Barney.

©The Research Foundation of the ICFA

Table 4.5   (Continued)

Fixed-Income Portfolio

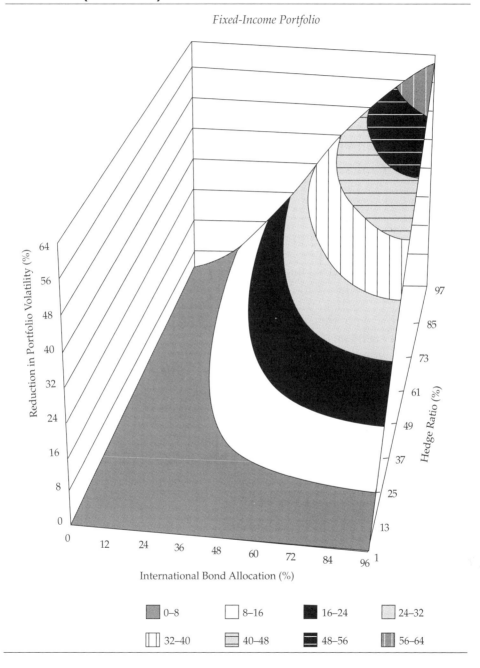

ing have a meaningful effect on portfolio volatility, and even this influence is modest when compared to the effect of hedging in a fixed-income portfolio.[8]

Managing return variability, however, is only part of the hedging issue. As already emphasized, no analysis can definitively determine that currency returns over a given strategic planning horizon will be either positive or zero; indeed, currency returns may be quite negative. The recommended 50 percent hedge ratio is, therefore, more of a response to the considerable uncertainty surrounding the direction of future exchange rate changes than it is a volatility-reduction strategy.[9]

Historical Implications of the 50 Percent Hedge Ratio. Because the 50 percent hedge ratio in developed international markets is a fundamental tenet of this monograph, an explanation of the historical implications of this approach is important. Although the relationship among hedged, unhedged, and 50 percent hedged returns is obviously linear, the relationship among the covariance matrixes is not, as shown in Table 4.3. A 50 percent hedged benchmark provided three-quarters of the volatility reduction and only half of the correlation increase of moving from unhedged to hedged returns. Regardless of the dollar regime, the risk–return tradeoff of this approach compares quite favorably with that of investing in the U.S. equity market and the correlation remains an attractive 0.50.

Figure 4.6 presents 50 percent hedged returns and standard deviations for each country for two halves of a 19-year sample period.[10] Because this illustration serves to provide familiarity with a return reporting convention that may be new to some, a few points merit mention:

- The U.S. market was less volatile than almost every international equity market in both subperiods. Currency returns were not entirely responsible for the higher standard deviation of returns in such large, well-established equity markets as France and the United Kingdom.
- Although the Japanese equity market has a well-deserved reputation for

---

[8]Given the magnitude of currency return volatility relative to bond return volatility, hedging significantly affects fixed-income portfolio volatility. Over the 1978–96 period, complete hedging would have eliminated more than 60 percent of the return volatility associated with an unhedged international bond portfolio.

[9]Because the focus in this discussion is on a global equity portfolio, hedging is discussed in that context. The implication is not that hedging should be handled separately in the equity and fixed-income pieces of a pension portfolio. Currency decisions should be made in the context of the entire portfolio.

[10]October 1987 is omitted from Figure 4.6 because of the impact it would have on this relatively small sample and because this date falls near the middle of the sample and thus could be included in either half of the sample. New Zealand, Finland, Ireland, and Malaysia do not appear because returns for these markets were first available in January 1988.

Table 4.3. MSCI EAFE Index versus the U.S. Equity Market by Currency Regime, January 1978–December 1996

Currency Regime	Local	Unhedged	Hedged[a]	50 Percent Hedged	United States
Total period (228 months)					
Average return	14.1%	16.7%	15.3%	16.0%	16.8%
Standard deviation	15.9%	20.1%	16.2%	17.2%	16.8%
Correlation with U.S.	0.55	0.42	0.55	0.50	—
Weak dollar (107 months)					
Average return	6.3%	24.7%	6.2%	15.1%	16.1%
Standard deviation	17.3%	23.5%	17.6%	19.7 %	19.1%
Correlation with U.S.	0.55	0.40	0.55	0.49	—
Strong dollar (121 months)					
Average return	21.5%	10.1%	23.9%	16.8%	17.4%
Standard deviation	13.7%	17.0 %	13.7%	14.7%	14.4%
Correlation with U.S.	0.57	0.47	0.56	0.53	—

[a]Hedging done on a one-month-forward, present-value basis.

Source: MSCI for local return data; Datastream International for exchange rates and short-term interest rates (some data on short-term interest rates from Goldman Sachs).

being volatile, a number of developed markets, such as Italy, Norway, Hong Kong, and Sweden, were even more volatile over each of the two subperiods.

- As well as markets have done in 1995 and 1996, the average return over the first subperiod was higher than that over the second subperiod in all 18 countries. In most cases, however, returns over the later period were less volatile.

Correlations

Since Markowitz (1959) introduced the portfolio variance equation, low correlations have represented the cornerstone of diversification.[11] Grubel (1968), Solnik (1974b), Levy and Sarnat (1970), and Lessard (1976) introduced U.S. investors to attractive gains from international diversification stemming from low correlations among the global equity markets. Although many subsequent studies have been conducted on this key component of international investing, three recent findings are particularly noteworthy:

- Over the past 37 years, equity market correlations have fluctuated widely but, on average, have risen only slightly.[12] This point is critical. Academics

---

[11] See also Markowitz (1991).

[12] Solnik, Boucrelle, and Le Fur (1996); Michaud et al. (1996).

Figure 4.6. Developed Equity Market Risk–Return Profile, January 1978–December 1996

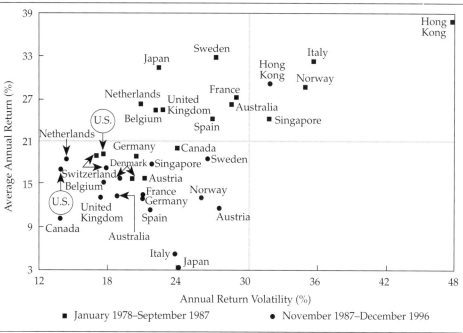

Source: Based on data from MSCI and Ibbotson Associates.

and practitioners alike have been unable to identify a significant, systematic, secular rise in correlations.

- Equity market correlations appear to increase during global economic slowdowns and to fall during expansions.[13]
- Equity market correlations appear to rise during periods of high return volatility and to fall during periods of low volatility.[14]

Sources of Intermarket Correlations. The attractive intermarket correlations have five principal sources: nonsynchronized economic and interest rate cycles (or fiscal and monetary policies); industry concentration differences; collective company-level idiosyncrasies; exchange rate translation; and the nature of benchmark construction. Although the combined effect of these sources certainly fluctuates over time, nothing supports the contention that some secular, systematic mitigation of these influences is underway. Even a watershed event such as the looming European Monetary Union (EMU) does not guarantee

---

[13] Strongin, Petsch, and Fenton (1997); Erb, Harvey, and Viskanta (1994).
[14] Longin and Solnik (1995); Erb, Harvey, and Viskanta (1994).

homogeneity for all five fronts. Intermarket correlations should persist at levels sufficient to support the case for international diversification.

▨ *Nonsynchronized fiscal and monetary policies.* The correlation of U.S. economic growth with that of other developed nations is neither stable over time nor particularly high on average, as indicated by Table 4.4. Canada is the one exception, and Table 4.5 reveals the reason.[15] International trade represents a relatively large proportion of Canadian gross national product (GNP), and the United States accounts for the vast majority of this commerce. As with Canada, international trade plays a much more significant role in the European economies than it does in either the United States or Japan, but the United States accounts for a relatively small part of European international commerce. In short, Table 4.4 is a simple means of demonstrating that, whereas non-U.S. developed markets are not completely insulated from the economic fortunes of the United States, these economies are by no means completely dependent on the United States.

The correlation of the U.S. interest rate cycle with the interest rate cycles of other developed nations is neither intertemporally stable (i.e., stable over time) nor close to unity, as indicated by Table 4.6. (Again, Canada is the one exception.) Relative to changes in GDP, however, the correlation of interest rate fluctuations is higher on average. Simply put, despite G–7 agreements

Table 4.4. Correlation of Quarterly U.S. Real GDP Growth with GDP Growth in Other Developed Markets, 1960–96

Decade	Japan	Germany	United Kingdom	France	Canada	Italy	Nether-lands	Switzer-land
1960s	–0.01	–0.10	0.17	NA	0.47	NA	NA	NA
1970s	0.42	0.07	0.25	NA	0.39	NA	NA	NA
1980s	0.20	0.30	0.19	0.12	0.62	0.26	0.27	0.17
1990s	–0.44	–0.32	0.60	0.33	0.65	0.10	0.12	0.09

NA = not available.

Source: Datastream International.

---

[15]Technically, to illustrate the linkages among economies, the trade statistics in Table 4.5 should be combined with in-country sales data that reflect the direct investment abroad by countries. For example, U.S. multinational firms sell considerably more products abroad through their affiliates than the U.S. economy exports. Further, the foreign affiliates export a substantial amount, some of which is imported into the United States. Such considerations would improve Table 4.5 but would not undermine the assertion that international economies are far from completely dependent upon the U.S. economy. (For a good discussion of U.S. in-country sales, see the Joseph P. Quinlan, "Global Engagement: Understanding How U.S. Companies Compete in the World Economy, " Morgan Stanley Dean Witter International Economics—U.S. and the Americas Investment Research (December 1997).

Table 4.5. U.S. Trading Activity, December 31, 1995

Country	Exports as a Share of GNP	U.S. Share of Exports (U.S. imports)	Imports as a Share of GNP	U.S. Share of Imports (U.S. exports)
G–9 Countries				
Canada	33.2%	78.0%	28.5%	77.2%
France	19.8	6.2	18.9	5.2
Germany	22.6	7.5	19.7	5.0
Italy	21.3	7.5	18.8	4.3
Japan	8.9	28.7	6.8	19.1
Netherlands	42.8	4.3	37.3	12.0
Switzerland	28.4	9.7	28.0	7.8
United Kingdom	21.9	11.6	24.0	11.0
United States	8.2	—	10.9	—
Other Major U.S. Trading Partners				
China	20.0%	32.6%	17.7%	8.9%
Korea	28.8	19.9	31.1	18.8
Mexico	26.2	78.6	23.8	62.6

Note: Top five U.S. trading partners are, in order, Canada, Japan, Mexico, China, and Germany.
Sources: International Monetary Fund and the IFC.

Table 4.6. Correlation of Quarterly U.S. Bond Yield Changes with Yield Changes in Other Developed Markets, 1960–96

Decade	Japan	Germany	United Kingdom	France	Canada	Italy	Nether-lands	Switzer-land
1960s	NA	0.17	0.16	0.14	0.50	−0.04	NA	NA
1970s	0.09	0.19	−0.05	0.30	0.67	0.07	0.26	0.18
1980s	0.53	0.59	0.36	0.56	0.91	0.23	0.62	0.64
1990s	0.65	0.56	0.65	0.55	0.83	−0.06	0.54	0.53

NA = not available.
Source: Ibbotson Associates and Datastream International.

and bilateral efforts with respect to exchange rates and trade, the fiscal and monetary policies of the United States are not perfectly coordinated with those of other countries. As a result, the economic growth and interest rate cycles of the United States diverge from those of other nations.

▓ *Industry concentration differences.* Correlations are also influenced by the industrial composition of countries. Industries differ in many ways. The bottom line is that industry-level returns (or in a broader sense, economic-sector returns) differ considerably for many reasons, and the representation of economic sectors varies widely among the developed and emerging markets, as suggested by Figure 4.7.

©The Research Foundation of the ICFA

Figure 4.7. Sector Concentration of MSCI World and IFC Investable Country Indexes, December 1996

(largest sector listed with bar)

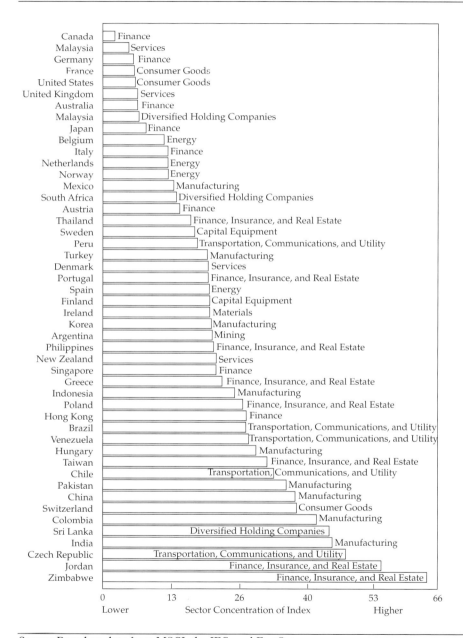

This figure is based on the Herfindahl Index, which is scaled so that it has a minimum value of zero (indicating an equal concentration in each of the eight or nine economic sectors) and a maximum value of 100 (indicating the presence of only one economic sector). The index is calculated as

$$\frac{\sum_{i=1}^{n} (\text{Sector representation})^2 - \frac{1}{n}}{1 - \frac{1}{n}},$$

where n is the number of sectors (MSCI World Index has eight; the IFC Investable Composite has nine).

Figure 4.7 highlights several points. First, the indexes of the G–5 (i.e., United States, United Kingdom, Japan, France, and Germany), Canada, Australia, and Malaysia are the most balanced in terms of sector exposure. Emerging markets are, on average, roughly half as diversified on an economic sector basis as the developed economies. The identity of the largest sector, however, varies significantly among all countries.

Second, high sector concentration is not exclusive to emerging markets. Switzerland has a higher sector concentration than 20 of the 26 emerging markets, and Hong Kong has less sector diversification than half of the emerging market indexes.

Third, the industry/sector exposures for a country in the emerging market indexes can differ considerably from the industry/sector exposures in the country's economy as a whole. Although such a situation can occur in any country, the problem is a major issue in emerging markets because of investability adjustments, the developing nature of the stock markets, and the effect of outsourcing by developed nations.

Finally, Malaysia appears twice because it is included in both the MSCI World Index and the IFC Investable Composite Index.[16] This fact can have unintended policy portfolio consequences. When a 5 percent IFC Investable position is added to an existing 15 percent MSCI EAFE Index position, the exposure to Malaysia increases from 0.4 percent to 1.5 percent, which exceeds

---

[16]MSCI initially combined Malaysia and Singapore in a single index. At that time, many of the largest Malaysian stocks traded on the Singapore Stock Exchange. As the years passed, however, Malaysian companies switched to the Kuala Lumpur Stock Exchange and the Malaysian and Singapore markets became more distinct. When MSCI officially separated the markets in its World Index in 1993, it concluded that, although Malaysia had been part of its emerging market indexes since 1988, dropping Malaysia from the World Index represented a change "too severe for both the Malaysian stock market and the international investors who were invested in Malaysian stocks." As a result, Malaysia currently appears in the MSCI developed *and* emerging market indexes.

the exposure to every other country except Japan and the United Kingdom. Because of the different index construction methodologies, the sector concentration is slightly higher in the IFC Malaysia Index than in the MSCI Malaysia Index.

▨ *Collective company-level idiosyncrasies.* Like industry concentration differences, company-specific risk represents a diversifiable risk that influences correlations. To appreciate fully the company-level source, however, one must understand the role of integration, as distinct from segmentation, in asset-pricing theory.

In an integrated global market, no barriers to investment exist and companies with the same risk are priced consistently in all markets. Conversely, a segmented global market is one in which legal restrictions, transaction costs, political risks, information asymmetries, exchange rate uncertainty, nationalistic tendencies, or a general discomfort/lack of familiarity with foreign markets inhibit capital flows *or* one in which securities with the same risk characteristics are valued differently by markets.

Given such definitions, integration is not synonymous with rising correlations and low correlations are not necessarily indicative of segmentation. Also, segmentation need not reflect inefficiency. In a segmented market, new information may be readily available, interpreted rationally, and discounted quickly. The local marginal-price setter simply may process some information in a unique manner.

If markets are assumed to be completely integrated, the "risk" (defined as return volatility) associated with a given stock can be defined as

$$\sigma_i^2 = \beta_{i,World}^2 \sigma_{World}^2 + \beta_{i,Country}^2 \sigma_{Country}^2 + \beta_{i,Industry}^2 \sigma_{Industry}^2 + \sigma_{Specific}^2,$$

where

$$\sigma_i^2 = \text{Variance of returns for stock } i$$

$$\beta_{i,World} = \frac{\sigma_{i,World}}{\sigma_{World}^2} = \frac{\text{Covariance of stock } i \text{ returns with world factor}}{\text{Variance of world factor}}$$

$$\beta_{i,Country} = \frac{\sigma_{i,Country}}{\sigma_{Country}^2} = \frac{\text{Covariance of stock } i \text{ returns with country factor}}{\text{Variance of country factor}}$$

$$\beta_{i,Industry} = \frac{\sigma_{i,Industry}}{\sigma_{Industry}^2} = \frac{\text{Covariance of stock } i \text{ returns with industry factor}}{\text{Variance of industry factor}}$$

$$\sigma_{Specific}^2 = \text{Variance of company-specific factor}$$

In this equation, $\beta_{i,\,World}^2\sigma_{World}^2$ represents systematic risk and the rest of the expression represents diversifiable risk.[17]

The essence of this formulation of risk is that by holding the world market portfolio, all diversifiable risks at the country, industry, and company levels are eliminated, leaving only systematic risk. Among the firms of a given industry, however, the nature of company-specific risk is such that correlations can be quite low. Table 4.7 shows that even stocks in the same industry with identical betas relative to the world market portfolio can have very low correlations with each other.

Such low correlations are attributable to a myriad of financial and business differences. For example, companies in the same industry differ in terms of return on equity, return on assets, operating leverage, financial leverage, reliance on imported inputs to production process, the significance of "strategic" relationships with the government or other firms, company size, labor intensity, labor union strength, the extent to which sales are spread among different product lines, and the degree to which revenues are derived from international versus domestic sources. Because the collective influence of these factors varies from one country to the next, correlations among firms in even the most globalized industries, such as oil, are well below one.

Note, however, that research has demonstrated that markets are only partially integrated and that the level of integration varies from one country to the next as a result of factors such as economic significance, political power, export activity, and the presence of multinational firms.[18] This finding is corroborated by readily observable evidence of segmentation—a domestic market bias in investment portfolios (integration would involve more globally diversified portfolios), a relatively high correlation between domestic investment and domestic savings (integration would involve a lower correlation because capital needs could be met from the global savings pool), and a relatively low correlation of consumption among markets (integration would involve more-homogenous consumption patterns). As a result, the previous definition of the risk associated with a given stock must be revised as

$$\sigma_i^2 = \beta_{i,\,World}^2\sigma_{World}^2 + \beta_{i,\,Country}^2\sigma_{Country}^2 + \beta_{i,\,Industry}^2\sigma_{Industry}^2 + \sigma_{Specific}^2,$$

---

[17]For conceptual purposes, this equation assumes that the factors are orthogonal. In reality, the world, country, and industry betas are not clearly differentiable. The industry factor will explain some fraction of the country factor and the country factor will explain some part of the world factor. The technical implication of such linear dependence in an ordinary least squares regression is that the betas, although they are the best linear unbiased estimators, may be imprecise.

[18]For example, see Beckers, Connor, and Curds (1996).

Table 4.7. Beta and Correlation in Industry X

	Annual Return				
	World	Stock 1	Stock 2	Stock 3	Stock 4
Year					
1	10.0%	7.0%	2.3%	20.0%	20.0%
2	20.0	15.0	7.0	20.0	20.0
3	5.0	2.0	4.2	1.1	20.0
4	1.0	2.5	4.0	3.7	1.2
5	3.0	14.0	−3.7	2.3	0.8
6	15.0	15.0	6.4	20.0	0.2
7	8.0	1.6	1.7	−0.1	19.3
8	0.0	−5.0	−3.9	12.3	−0.2
9	−3.0	12.0	−4.1	20.0	12.6
10	6.0	0.9	−3.9	0.7	6.1
Return statistics					
Average	6.5%	6.5%	1.0%	10.0%	10.0%
Standard deviation	6.7%	6.7%	4.3%	8.8%	8.8%
Beta relative to world		0.47	0.47	0.47	0.47
Correlation[a]					
World	1.00				
Stock 1	0.46	1.00			
Stock 2	0.74	0.31	1.00		
Stock 3	0.36	0.53	0.25	1.00	
Stock 4	0.36	0.06	0.35	0.11	1.00

[a]The correlation (ρ_{xy}) between two assets (x and y) is

$$\rho_{xy} = \frac{\sum_{i=1}^{n} p_i (R_{xi} - \bar{R}_x)(R_{yi} - \bar{R}_y)}{\sqrt{\sum_{i=1}^{n} p_i (R_{xi} - \bar{R}_x)^2 \sum_{i=1}^{n} P_i (R_{yi} - \bar{R}_y)^2}} = \frac{\sigma_{xy}}{\sigma_x \sigma_y},$$

where R is return, p is the probability of the ith return occurring, σ is standard deviation, and σ_{xy} is covariance. So, correlation is a function of return volatility and return covariance.

where $\beta_{i,\,World}^2 \sigma_i^2 + \beta_{i,\,Country}^2 \sigma_{Country}^2$ represents systematic risk and the rest of the equation is diversifiable risk. The existence of a country-level systematic risk component can compound the aforementioned aggregate firm influences, thereby producing lower intermarket correlations than would exist in a fully integrated financial marketplace.

The strength of this country-level risk factor is the reason that shares of U.S. multinational firms have been abandoned as a cost-effective means of gaining international equity exposure. For example, Jacquillat and Solnik (1978) demonstrated that the international component of U.S. multinational firms' return variability accounts for less than 2 percent of total return variability and concluded that not much difference exists between the shares of U.S. multinational firms and those of domestically oriented U.S. companies.[19]

  Exchange rate translation. Currency return volatility is determined by factors such as reported inflation, changing inflation expectations, fluctuations in the real exchange rate, and the activities of monetary authorities. Differences among countries in the variability of these factors and in the relationship between these factors and local equity returns affect the intermarket correlations experienced by an unhedged U.S. investor. (Note that hedged investors do not completely avoid the effect of exchange rate changes—for two reasons. First, some residual exchange rate risk is associated with hedged portfolios. Although the current value of an equity portfolio can be protected against currency volatility, the future return on that portfolio obviously is unknown and cannot be hedged. Second, currency volatility directly affects local equity return volatility and cross-market correlations. Stock prices among countries exhibit varying degrees of sensitivity to fluctuations in exchange rates.)[20]

  Table 4.8 summarizes the role played by exchange rates in select equity

Table 4.8. Effect of Currency on International Equity Correlations with U.S. Equity, January 1992–December 1996
(annualized statistics)

Currency Exposure	Japan	Germany	United Kingdom	Canada	Switzerland	Australia
Hedged (US$) equity volatility	20.6%	14.3%	12.7%	11.6%	13.1%	13.4%
Hedged equity correlations with U.S. equity	0.22	0.35	0.49	0.60	0.40	0.53
Currency volatility (US$)	10.6%	10.3%	10.6%	4.4%	12.2%	7.2%
Currency correlation with hedged equity	−0.01	−0.45	−0.30	0.18	−0.39	0.28
Unhedged (US$) equity volatility	23.0%	13.3%	13.8%	13.1%	14.1%	16.9%
Unhedged equity correlation with U.S. equity	0.12	0.29	0.50	0.60	0.23	0.49

Note: Because volatility and covariance jointly determine correlation, standard deviations are presented along with correlations.
Source: MSCI.

---

[19] See also Senchack and Beedles (1980).
[20] See Roll (1992).

market correlations realized by U.S. investors over the 1992–96 period and illustrates three important points. First, currency exposure typically reduces the correlation between international and U.S. equity returns, but this effect is not always true, as the data for the United Kingdom demonstrate. Second, considerable variation can occur in the volatility of currency returns and in the relationship between local equity returns and exchange rate changes. In this example, standard deviations ranged from 4.4 percent to 12.2 percent and correlations ranged from –0.45 to 0.28. Finally, as a result of such variation, although unhedged returns are typically more volatile than hedged returns, exceptions do occur, as the data for Germany indicate.

▨ *Nature of benchmark construction.* Considerable differences exist among the various country-level indexes in terms of the number and type of constituent companies, as indicated by the benchmark comparison among MSCI World Index countries in Table 3.3 and the benchmark comparison among emerging markets in Table 3.6. Hence, the index construction methodology can affect intermarket correlations.

With the principal sources of correlation as a conceptual backdrop, consider the historical correlations between the U.S. equity market and 50 percent hedged developed equity markets shown in Figure 4.8. If correlations fluctuate through time in a random manner, the points in Figure 4.8 should be scattered on either side of the diagonal line. The greater the vertical distance between a given point and the diagonal, the greater was the change in correlation between the two periods. For example, the U.K. point lies well off the diagonal. The correlation between the United States and the United Kingdom over the first half of the sample was 0.50, but it increased to 0.68 over the second half. Conversely, the correlation between Japan and the United States did not change much (0.20 versus 0.27) so the Japan point is reasonably close to the diagonal.

Figure 4.8 thus illustrates three points: First, on average, a modest rise occurred in the correlation between international developed and U.S. equity markets in the past two decades; the differences between the two periods, however, are quite consistent with the long-term historical volatility of correlation coefficients. In other words, investors can only speculate on whether this phenomenon is transitory or secular, because historical data offer many examples of correlations that rose in one period only to fall in the next. Second, the correlation of non-U.S. markets with the U.S. equity market remains far from unity. Third, partially hedged international equity markets continue to provide attractive diversification benefits relative to traditional U.S. investments, such as investment-grade bonds and small-capitalization stocks.

Conditional Correlations. As already mentioned, a number of studies

Figure 4.8. Equity Return Correlations of 50 Percent Hedged Developed Equity Markets with the U.S. Equity Market, January 1978–December 1996

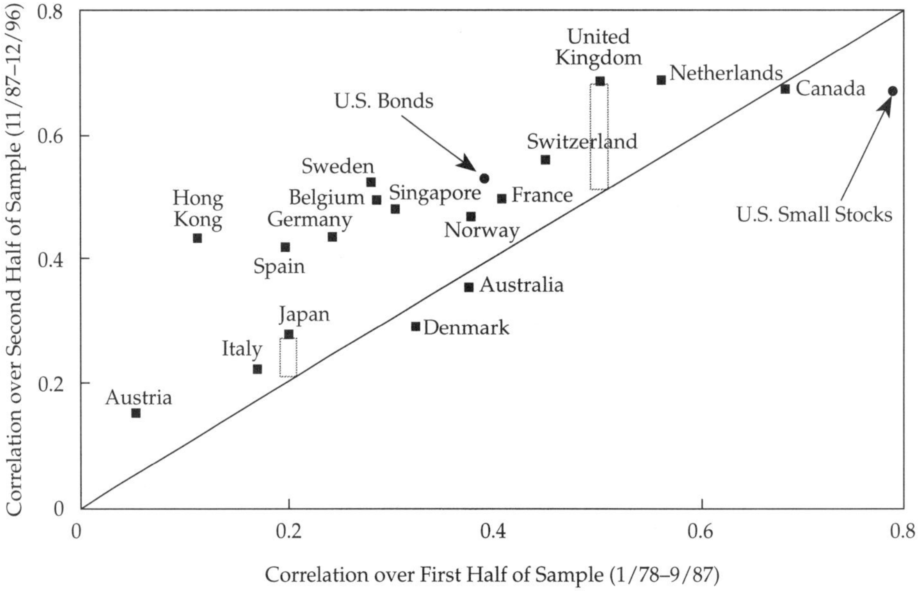

Source: Based on data from MSCI and Ibbotson Associates.

have analyzed the correlation between U.S. and international equity returns in different economic and return-volatility states. Some of these studies concluded that correlations increase when the U.S. market performs poorly and, therefore, international diversification fails when it is needed most. Although the efforts to better understand conditional correlations are important, such conclusions are often misinterpreted.

Consider the disaggregation of the correlation between U.S. equity returns and the partially hedged equity returns of the remaining G–9 countries (i.e., G–7 plus Switzerland and the Netherlands) shown in Table 4.9. Monthly returns are divided into three states.[21] For the first state, "both below average," the monthly U.S. return is below its average for the sample period, and

---

[21]Because returns are conditioned on the means for the entire sample period in Table 4.9, the covariance and variance calculations within each of the states are also based on these means. In other words, unconditional means are used instead of the different means within each state— the conditional means. This approach produces results that are directly comparable with the correlation for the entire period and, hence, are more consistent with intuition. For example, the "both above average" correlation is never lower than the correlation for the entire period.

Table 4.9   Conditional Correlations between U.S. and International Developed Equity Monthly Returns, January 1970– December 1996

State of Returns	Canada	France	Germany	Italy	Japan	Nether-lands	Switzer-land	United Kingdom
Both below average	0.84	0.82	0.83	0.74	0.77	0.87	0.85	0.83
Normal prior	0.82	0.75	0.70	0.68	0.69	0.79	0.77	0.77
Mixed	−0.56	−0.61	−0.62	−0.59	−0.53	−0.47	−0.57	−0.65
Normal prior	−0.52	−0.59	−0.59	−0.60	−0.56	−0.55	−0.54	−0.53
Both above average	0.81	0.68	0.60	0.60	0.64	0.74	0.72	0.67
Normal prior	0.82	0.75	0.70	0.68	0.69	0.79	0.77	0.77
Entire sample	0.71	0.46	0.38	0.23	0.29	0.61	0.57	0.54

Note: 324 months of 50 percent hedged returns. Expected and actual proportion of months in each state is approximately 33.3 percent. Local returns were used to represent hedged returns prior to 1978 because hedging preserves the local return covariance matrix.
Source: MSCI.

the return in the non-U.S. country is also below its sample average. In the "mixed" state, the monthly U.S. return is above its average and the monthly return of the other market is below its average, or vice versa. In the "both above average" state, both monthly returns are above their respective sample means.[22]

To put each of the conditional correlations in the proper perspective, a normal prior is provided. This prior was generated via a Monte Carlo simulation, assuming all return distributions are normal with a correlation equal to the entire-period (or unconditional) level. Because a positive correlation of any magnitude produces high correlations, when returns are parsed as in Table 4.9, the normal prior represents the correlation that is completely consistent with the entire-period correlation and reflects symmetric investor reactions to positive and negative shocks to the financial marketplace.

The results in Table 4.9 are consistent with the commonly cited evidence that diversification fails when it is needed most. Correlations in the both-below-average state are higher than expected, whereas correlations in the both-above-average state are lower than expected. By definition, the observed and normal prior correlations in each of these states differ in a statistically significant manner from the entire-period correlation. No significance can be assigned, however, to the average 10 percent difference between the observed and expected values within each of the two states. Concluding that interna-

---

[22]This method of parsing returns was used in Erb, Harvey, and Viskanta (1994).

tional diversification systematically has provided a benefit less than that suggested by long-term correlations is a misinterpretation of the results.

A more conventional method of grouping return data, in which groups are determined simply according to the level of U.S. returns, is shown in Table 4.10. The correlations in most of the categories diverge modestly from the normal priors in a manner similar to those in Table 4.9. Unlike the previous approach, however, the proportion of observations in the "outlier" categories is small and asymmetric. Specifically, the correlation in the "less than –5 percent" category is quite sensitive to a single observation and, therefore, may differ significantly from the normal prior as a result of small-sample bias. (Only 21 such instances have occurred in the past 27 years, whereas the "greater than 5 percent" state includes twice as many instances.)

Note that such studies, by their very nature, pertain to tactical, not strategic, asset allocation. Strategic asset allocation focuses on long-term expected values, but this type of conditional work focuses on the aggregation of short-term departures from those averages. In the context of long-term positive correlations, a belief that the U.S. equity market will drop sharply during the next month obviously implies a view that the likelihood of international equity markets underperforming their respective expected returns is

Table 4.10. Conditional Correlations between U.S. and International Developed Equity Monthly Returns, January 1970– December 1996

Level of U.S. Returns	Canada	France	Germany	Italy	Japan	Nether-lands	Switzer-land	United Kingdom
Less than –5 percent	0.87	0.75	0.80	0.60	0.66	0.92	0.88	0.92
Normal prior	0.88	0.73	0.67	0.40	0.55	0.79	0.79	0.75
–2 percent to –5 percent	0.74	0.57	0.43	0.17	0.32	0.69	0.67	0.44
Normal prior	0.75	0.49	0.38	0.21	0.23	0.58	0.62	0.56
–2 percent to 2 percent	0.32	0.17	0.07	0.04	0.11	0.23	0.16	0.11
Normal prior	0.34	0.17	0.17	0.14	0.14	0.30	0.23	0.22
2 percent to 5 percent	0.54	0.17	0.17	–0.02	0.15	0.41	0.34	0.23
Normal prior	0.56	0.28	0.27	0.17	0.19	0.39	0.39	0.32
Greater than 5 percent	0.84	0.63	0.35	0.38	0.28	0.63	0.57	0.59
Normal prior	0.83	0.58	0.49	0.32	0.41	0.77	0.71	0.70
Entire sample	0.71	0.46	0.38	0.23	0.29	0.61	0.57	0.54

Note: 324 months of 50 percent hedged returns. Local returns were used to represent hedged returns prior to 1978 because hedging preserves the local return covariance matrix.
Source: MSCI.

considerably greater than average, which is a tactical consideration. Such a belief indicates nothing about the appropriateness of the strategic correlation assumptions that encompass all of the return states in Table 4.9 and Table 4.10.

In summary, the evidence in these two tables is not a death knell for diversification because the *statistical* evidence is simply too weak. The *anecdotal* evidence permits debate to continue on whether differences between actual experience and normal prior are attributable to sampling error or to some behavioral phenomenon. Perhaps human nature is such that investors tend to respond most uniformly to really bad news. Only time will settle that debate.

Final Note on Correlations. Although the diversification benefit of emerging market equity has been well advertised, a worthwhile point to consider is the difference between emerging and partially hedged developed equity markets in terms of their correlation with the U.S. market. Figure 4.9 shows that correlations for the emerging markets were half the size of those for the developed markets over the second subperiod established in Figure 4.8 (November 1987–December 1996). On a capitalization-weighted basis, the correlations were 0.23 for emerging and 0.46 for developed markets.

A more important point is to acknowledge the considerable diversification benefits offered by international equity relative to any U.S. equity benchmark. U.S. plan sponsors often spend a great deal of time worrying about the composition of their U.S. equity portfolio and weighing such considerations as the appropriate blend of value and growth or the proper capitalization mix. Although such considerations are important, they pale in comparison with the diversification benefits offered by international equity relative to any U.S. equity benchmark, as demonstrated by Figure 4.10. The decisions made with respect to global equity allocations will have a far more significant impact on portfolio performance than will refinements to the U.S. equity allocation.

Costs of International Equity Investing

The fact that investing in international equities is more expensive than investing in U.S. equities is common knowledge. The prospect of higher transaction and custody costs, steeper management fees, and dividend withholding taxes provides some investors with ample reason to avoid international diversification. Unfortunately, these investors often fail to appreciate either the rate at which costs have fallen over the past few years or the subtleties of the cost data. Custody and clearing costs illustrate the reduction of costs, and dividend withholding taxes provide an excellent example of the nuances of the data.

Custody and Clearing Costs. An estimate of the custody, clearing, and management costs associated with international and U.S. equity mandates is

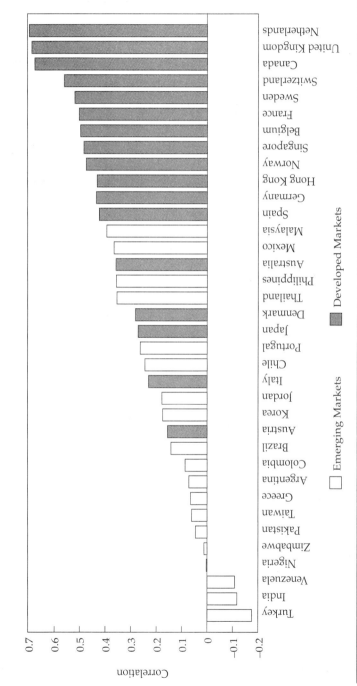

Figure 4.9. Ranking of Correlations between Various International Markets and the U.S. Equity Market, November 1987–December 1996

Source: Based on data from MSCI and the IFC.

Figure 4.10. Correlations between Various Benchmarks and MSCI U.S. Index, November 1987–December 1996

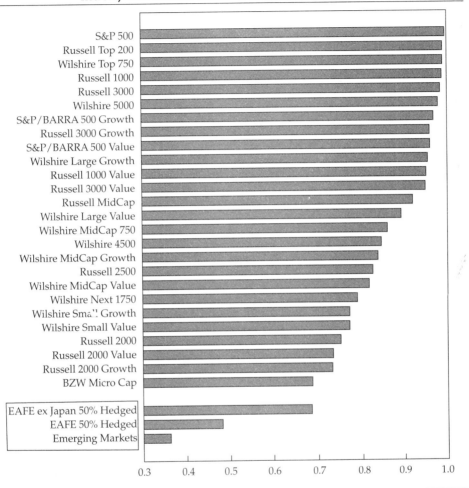

Source: Ibbotson Associates.

provided in Table 4.11 for the second quarter of 1997. The situation-specific nature of these costs prevents the use of a single estimate that applies to all institutions, and the data in Table 4.11, though conservative, should be viewed in this context.

The custody and clearing costs in Table 4.11 are characterized by economies of scale (i.e., fees are inversely proportional to portfolio value) and reflect no special relationship with the custodial bank that might reduce these charges. The custodian receives a fee that is a function of three portfolio characteristics—country exposures, size, and the number of holdings. The

Table 4.11. International Equity Costs
(annual basis points)

Portfolio Mandate and Costs	Portfolio Size ($ millions)		
	$50	$100	$200
U.S. equity			
Custody, clearing, and trading costs[a]	25	24	24
Management fees	55	48	42
Total	80	72	66
50 Percent hedged EAFE equity			
Custody, clearing, and trading costs[b]	91	76	69
Management fees	67	58	53
Total	158	134	122
Increment to U.S. equity	78	62	56
Emerging market equity			
Custody, clearing, and trading costs	185	177	175
Management fees	110	105	100
Total	295	282	275
Increment to U.S. equity	215	210	209

Note: Estimates are for an actively managed portfolio.

[a]Estimates reflect the trading cost differences in Table 4.12.

[b]Estimates reflect the additional 20–30 bps in cost of managing a partially hedged portfolio. The sources of this cost range from the bid–ask spread on forward contracts to the costs associated with buying and selling securities to manage the cash flows related to forward contracts.

Sources: Data on custody and clearing costs from Putnam Investments and State Street Bank; data on management fees from Callan Associates, "Management Fee Survey" (May 1997) and Putnam Investments.

custodial bank also charges a transaction fee associated with the settlement of trades. Obviously, the level of turnover in the portfolio and the countries in which the trading occurs are the primary determinants of this cost.[23]

The extent to which the transaction fee can vary is indicated by Table 4.12, which presents a country-level trading cost supplement to the data in Table 4.11.[24] Three important points can be drawn from Table 4.12. First, trading in emerging markets is typically five times as expensive as trading in the United

---

[23]The assumptions in Table 4.11 concerning security turnover and the total number of holdings in the portfolio reflect the actual experience of conventional institutional accounts.

[24]In reviewing Table 4.12, keep the following two points in mind. First, the spreads obviously will increase (in some cases considerably) during times of market stress or for relatively large trades. Second, the spreads represent an approximation of market impact (the change in price between the time a broker receives an order and execution). Although the accuracy of this approximation varies from market to market, the cap-weighted spread is actually quite close to the cap-weighted impact as estimated by the Plexus Group, "Multinational Equity Trade Review" (First quarter, 1997).

Table 4.12. Global Equity Transaction Costs, Second Quarter 1997
(annual basis points)

Country	Physical Stock Transaction Costs				Futures
	Spread	Taxes	Commission	Total Costs[a]	Total[b]
United States	43	0	8	51	10
Germany	34	0	19	53	11
France	36	0	20	56	12
Netherlands	40	0	22	62	31
Sweden	41	0	23	64	54
Spain	43	0	22	65	22
Canada	54	0	19	73	26
Switzerland	36	18	21	74	29
Italy	55	0	22	76	16
Belgium	50	0	28	78	
Denmark	85	0	28	113	
Finland	73	0	43	116	
New Zealand	77	0	40	117	
Hong Kong	62	32	23	117	22
Australia	62	30	27	119	12
Japan	84	21	15	120	11
Norway	92	0	33	125	
Austria	92	0	55	147	
United Kingdom	90	50	12	152	11
Israel	102	0	77	179	
South Africa	101	50	45	196	
Malaysia	113	10	75	198	
Singapore	106	10	85	201	
Portugal	105	10	88	203	
Mexico	178	0	50	228	
Argentina	123	32	76	231	
Brazil	145	5	85	235	
Korea	104	60	78	242	
Taiwan	87	30	130	247	
Pakistan	150	0	100	250	
Ireland	124	100	27	251	
Thailand	177	0	93	269	
Turkey	217	0	75	292	
Peru	188	0	128	316	
Indonesia	198	30	88	316	
Philippines	165	60	93	318	

Table 4.12. (Continued)

| Country | Physical Stock Transaction Costs | | | | Futures |
	Spread	Taxes	Commission	Total Costs[a]	Total[b]
Greece	178	60	115	353	
Russia	260	0	100	360	
China	200	60	105	365	
Czech Republic	194	25	147	366	
India	130	51	200	381	
Venezuela	159	50	180	389	
Sri Lanka	150	50	250	450	

Note: G–9 countries are highlighted.

[a]Roundtrip estimates for $200 million cap-weighted portfolio. Actual experience will depend on the position of brokers when portfolio trades are sent out to bid (i.e., whether brokers can internally cross—i.e., use their own trading books/inventory—most of the names or must go into the local market) and on whether or not the investment manager has success using crossing networks such as POSIT (the United States) or ITG (Japan and the United Kingdom).
[b]Roundtrip estimates for quarterly holding period (i.e., monthly contracts must be rolled twice). The Netherlands and Switzerland contracts are not approved by the Commodity Futures Trading Commission and must be traded synthetically.

Sources: Morgan Stanley, Goldman Sachs, Merrill Lynch & Company, and Salomon Smith Barney.

States. In some instances, however, using American Depositary Receipts (ADRs) or Global Depositary Receipts (GDRs), which indicates a multicountry placement, can reduce the costs associated with international investing. For example, ADRs may offer better liquidity than local shares, with no trading taxes or fixed commissions. Such instruments, however, are far from a panacea.[25]

Second, stamp and excise taxes make considerable contributions to total trading costs in some countries, such as the United Kingdom.

Finally, trading futures is *significantly* less expensive than transacting in the physical securities. For example, the ratio of total physical cost to futures cost is 15:1 in the United Kingdom. Note, however, that in some Asian markets, swaps provide the principal cost-effective alternative to transacting in the physical securities.

Management fees, like custody costs, reflect economies of scale. These fees depend on whether a portfolio is managed as a segmented account or as part of a commingled account. In a commingled account, "small" portfolios ($100 million or less) are pooled together under a single set of guidelines to provide the investment manager with economies of scale in administration and client service. In return, some investment managers will charge the same published fee that applies to a comparably sized segmented account but will

---

[25]See Peterson (1996).

absorb the custody and clearing costs shown in Table 4.11. Not long ago, this benefit was unavailable to plan sponsors because of such factors as less competition among investment managers, inferior technology, and a less developed global marketplace. Today, however, commingled accounts have reduced the expense impediment to international investing.

Although accounts of any size can negotiate management fees, "large" portfolios (greater than $100 million) are generally the ones that find they can negotiate a sufficiently low fee to justify a segmented account. Portfolios of this size also tend to demand more customization in terms of product and servicing than is available in a commingled structure. Negotiated fees (flat fees or, less typically, performance-based fees) vary widely for reasons ranging from the strategic value of a potential client to the perceived administrative demands of the client. As a result, the management fees depicted in Table 4.11 for portfolios more than $100 million may be considerably overstated.

In summary, the marginal costs of international investing relative to U.S. investing have fallen markedly in recent years and no longer present the same obstacle to diversifying abroad that they once did.

Dividend Withholding Taxes. Although the analysis of custody and clearing costs demonstrates the inappropriateness of relying on dated perceptions of cost as a reason to avoid international diversification, the following discussion of dividend withholding taxes illustrates that one must take the time to thoroughly understand often convoluted issues before applying popular representations of cost.

Since MSCI introduced its "net dividend" indexes, dividend withholding taxes have been one of the most publicized costs associated with international investing.[26] At conferences, many speakers mention that they used the net dividend series in their analyses to represent properly the returns that U.S. investors realized. Although the intent of such speakers is noble enough, the statement is incorrect. MSCI, partially in the interest of its international client base and partially to be conservative, calculates net dividend indexes from the perspective of a Luxembourg holding company. The applicable tax rates, except for the United Kingdom, are considerably higher than those actually faced by a U.S. investor, as shown in Figure 4.11.

The withholding taxes encountered by U.S. investors in developed and emerging markets, as well as the dividends to which these tax rates are

---

[26]Of course, when taxes make cash dividends unattractive to a large enough percentage of the shareholder base, companies find alternative means (e.g., share buybacks, stock dividends) of delivering benefits to their shareholders, as has occurred in the United States. As a result, the income component of total equity return dwindles as does the significance of dividend taxes.

Figure 4.11. MSCI "Net of Dividend Withholding Tax" Index, as of December 31, 1996

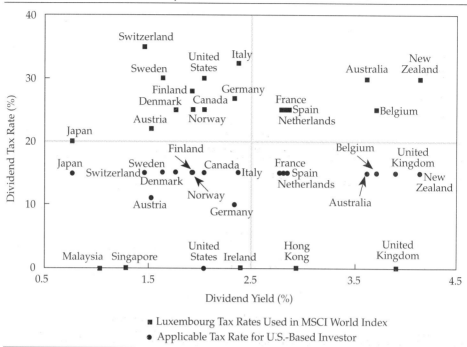

Source: Based on data from MSCI and the Bureau of Fiscal Documentation.

applied, are shown in Figure 4.12. An estimate of the annual impact of these taxes is provided in Table 4.13, which indicates that for a global portfolio, excluding the United States, the withholding tax is approximately 28 bps per year.

The dividend withholding tax story, however, does not end with Table 4.13. Even with the revisions to the data in Figure 4.11, Table 4.13 overstates the impact for three reasons.

First, tax treaties exist to prevent double taxation of dividends. U.S. investors receive net dividends as well as tax credits to apply against their U.S. tax on the gross dividends. These credits are obviously useless to pension funds, but pension funds often can reclaim some or all of the withholding taxes. (This process can be arduous, but because the custodian is responsible for dividend withholding tax reclamation, the logistical headaches associated with reclamation reside with that party and not the plan sponsor.) Furthermore, institutions occasionally can obtain exemptions from withholding taxes.

Second, in many of the developed markets, the withholding tax can be avoided completely by purchasing the futures contracts listed in Table 4.12.

Figure 4.12. Global Dividend Withholding Taxes Applicable to U.S. Investors, December 31, 1996

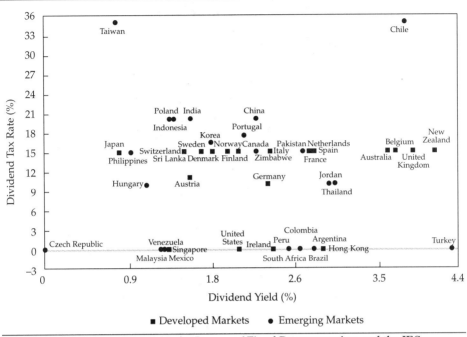

■ Developed Markets   ● Emerging Markets

Source: Based on data from MSCI, the Bureau of Fiscal Documentation, and the IFC.

Arbitrage occurs at the local level, so the full value of the dividend is factored into the futures price.

Third, on a more subtle level, properly assessing the dividend withholding tax issue is rarely as simple as applying a tax rate to a reported dividend yield, as was done for Table 4.13. The tax statutes tend to be complicated, and they are subject to revision (e.g., the United Kingdom in June 1997). For example, consider the specifics of the withholding tax in three of the largest MSCI EAFE Index countries, as follows:[27]

▒   *France—avoir fiscal.* The French government remits a cash payment as a credit for French taxes paid by corporations. The MSCI gross dividend includes this payment and, therefore, can approach 150 percent of the gross dividends reported by French companies. U.S. shareholders receive this cash payment, so the withholding tax counteracts government-sponsored supplements to dividends.[28] The effective reduction in the declared dividend itself is

---

[27]See Raahil R. Bengali and Sandy C. Rattray, "The Seasonality of Calendar Spreads in Europe: Effects of Taxation and Dividends on Futures Mispricing," Goldman Sachs Equity Derivatives Research (April 1996).

Table 4.13. Annual Effect of Dividend Withholding Tax, December 31, 1996

Tax Rates/Dividend Yield	MSCI EAFE	MSCI World	IFC Investable
Tax rates			
MSCI-reported Luxembourg rates	0.32%	0.45%	—
Applicable U.S. rates	0.29	0.16	0.14%
Dividend yield	2.15	2.10	2.03

Note: Does not include reinvestment effect, which is a function of dividend yield, capital appreciation, and holding period.

Sources: MSCI, the IFC, and Bureau of Fiscal Documentation.

smaller than the tax rate implies.

▓ *Germany—Steuerguthaben.* German residents receive a tax credit that they use when filing to reduce their tax burden. The MSCI gross dividend index includes this credit and, therefore, can approach 140 percent of the gross dividends reported by German companies. None of this benefit applies to U.S. shareholders, so one must be careful about applying the tax rate to an inflated base.

▓ *United Kingdom—Advance Corporation Tax.* U.K. companies declare and pay a net dividend (currently 80 percent), but MSCI reports the entire gross dividend. Prior to June 1997, local pension funds could reclaim in cash from tax authorities 25 percent of the net dividend received (i.e., the remaining 20 percent of the gross dividend) and U.S. tax-exempt institutions received 5 percent of the gross dividend from U.K. tax authorities, which made the effective withholding tax 15 percent for such institutions. Under the July 1997 Labour government budget, U.K. pension funds can reclaim none of the withholding, and U.S. plans will be similarly affected in 1999.[29]

Given these considerations, the actual impact of dividend withholding taxes on a U.S. pension plan is estimated to be 15 bps a year for non-U.S. developed markets and 10 bps a year for emerging markets. Adding these costs to those in Table 4.11 yields the total incremental international equity cost estimates in Table 4.14.

Summary. The cost estimates shown in Table 4.14, although nontrivial, are lower than is widely perceived. Nonetheless, they will have a significant bearing on the frequency and nature of tactical asset allocation statements.

---

[28]Source: MSCI and International Bureau of Fiscal Documentation.

[29]See Sandy C. Rattray, "Anatomy of a Change in the U.K. Dividend Tax: Points of Impact," Goldman Sachs Equity Derivatives Research (July 1997).

Table 4.14. Additional Annual Cost of International over U.S. Equity
(basis points)

	Portfolio Size ($ millions)		
Portfolio	$50	$100	$200
50 Percent hedged EAFE equity (from Table 4.10)	78	62	56
+Dividend withholding tax impact	29	29	29
−Adjustment for tax considerations	−14	−14	−14
Total	93	77	71
Emerging market equity (Table 3.11)	215	210	209
+Dividend withholding tax impact	14	14	14
−Adjustment for tax considerations	−4	−4	−4
Total	225	220	219

From a policy perspective, however, costs are not sufficiently high relative to the potential size of return differences among global equity markets to undermine the strategic case for international equity.

Conclusion

In addressing the three "C's" of international investing (currency, correlations, and costs), this chapter takes aim at some popular misconceptions. With respect to currency, using unhedged benchmarks is a common practice. This chapter, however, argues strongly for a 50 percent strategic hedge ratio because of the three- to five-year planning horizon of most plan sponsors, frequent significant and protracted deviations from equilibrium exchange rates, the lack of academic consensus on hedging policy, and the often overstated protection provided by a diversified basket of currencies. With respect to correlations, investors frequently point to increasing global integration and conditional correlation analyses as undermining the case for international diversification. This chapter contends that equating increasing global integration with rising correlations is a gross oversimplication and that fretting about diversification failing when it is needed most is a misinterpretation of the results of conditional correlation analyses. Finally, the costs associated with international investing often are perceived as prohibitively high. When properly demystified and tallied, these costs are lower than many expect but are still nontrivial. This fact, however, is something of a red herring, because cost differences continue to contract and return differences between U.S. and international equity markets over a three- to five-year period probably will be large enough (in one direction or the other) to render cost a moot point.

5. Conclusion

After a thorough review of the key issues of benchmarks, currency, correlations, and costs, the thesis of this monograph can be reiterated. Any reasonable set of forward-looking assumptions supports a significant strategic commitment to international equity, and critically, the immense uncertainty associated with prospective statements regarding equity market returns necessitates such a commitment. The latter point is basic yet seldom fully appreciated. The inability to predict the future represents the raison d'être of meaningful international diversification and a 50 percent hedge ratio. The typical U.S. pension plan, therefore, remains underexposed to international equity. The following allocation ranges generally represent more-appropriate strategic targets:

| | Global Equity Portfolio | | Portfolio with 60 Percent Equity | |
	Typical	Recommended	Typical	Recommended
U.S. equity	84%	45–70%	50%	27–42%
International developed market equity	15	25–40	9	15–24
Emerging market equity	1	5–15	1	3–9

Appendix

The following material expands on the discussion of the simulation in Chapter 2.

Major Equity Markets

The simulation discussed in Chapter 2 used only the three broad equity classes—U.S., international developed, and emerging—because of the conventions of the investment industry and the fact that graphical depiction of the simulation results is limited to three dimensions. The concept of international equity as an asset class, however, is an artifact of convenience, and plan sponsors should consider treating the major non-U.S. markets individually, as the United States is typically treated.

Given the significance of Germany, Japan, France, and the United Kingdom in benchmarks and given the high correlation between a market-capitalization-weighted portfolio of the remaining developed markets and any reasonable combination of these four countries, the strategic statements made concerning these countries will be the principal determinants of international equity performance. Recall that this notion was introduced in "Beyond Conventional Performance Benchmarks" in Chapter 2. Assuming the process responsible for producing strategic forecasts has some information content, adjustments made to the equilibrium allocations for the G–5 countries will be a value-adding activity. Strategic statements for these countries can be enhanced further by making benchmark-independent style trade-offs (i.e., value versus growth, small versus large capitalization). Note that these contentions in no way change the findings in this monograph. Results supporting a broadly defined asset class will only be strengthened by relaxing benchmark-imposed constraints on country weight and style bias.

Other Asset Classes

The focus of Chapter 2 is on a global equity portfolio. Obviously, the optimal allocations and marginal-benefit calculations will change if the optimization incorporates the many asset classes typically present in a pension portfolio. Because the three equity classes have relatively similar volatility, however, the global equity diversification recommended in this monograph is largely unaltered by the inclusion of assets such as U.S. investment-grade bonds, U.S. high-yield bonds, international developed market bonds, and emerging market bonds (based on an optimization volatility anchor of a 60 percent U.S. stock and 40 percent U.S. bond portfolio).

The impact of alternative investments is more ambiguous. The term "alternative investments" does not represent an asset class per se but rather is a catch-all category for a myriad of investments possessing one or more particular characteristics (private, illiquid, and nontraditional). This category includes domestic and international private equity (venture capital, buyouts, mezzanine financing, and industry- or geographically targeted investments), real estate (direct investments in commercial; industrial; hotel; retail; multi-family properties; and to a certain extent, publicly traded vehicles, such as equity or hybrid real estate investment trusts), private placements, bank loans, venture lending, commodities (e.g., precious metals, Goldman Sachs Commodity Index futures contracts), and hedge funds.[1]

The extensive array of choices and the importance of manager selection render impossible any generalizations about the impact of alternative investments on the recommended global equity portfolio. For example, assumptions regarding the return, volatility, and correlations associated with venture capital are often similar to those for emerging market equity, so these investments tend to compete with one another for space in the strategic portfolio. Conversely, investments such as commercial timberland investments, commodities, and many hedge funds offer sufficiently unique diversification benefits that they do not materially change the relative attractiveness of the three major equity classes.

Liabilities

A plan sponsor weighs three major factors in establishing a policy portfolio. The first consideration is the typical institutional portfolio. As discussed in Chapter 2, the lure of consensus portfolio positioning is strong. Most plan sponsors simply cannot wait 10–20 years for an unconventional investment policy to be validated. As a result, very few pension portfolios differ significantly from a 60 percent equity/40 percent bond mix. Such positioning certainly is not the result of identical return expectations, risk tolerance, or liability structure.

The second portfolio consideration is the asset-only analysis, in which a mean–variance or downside-risk optimization converts return, covariance, and risk-tolerance assumptions into a portfolio structure. A plan sponsor most

---

[1]Hedge funds are limited partnerships that were introduced as hedges against losses in traditional stock and bond portfolios. Hedge fund styles vary widely and include event-driven investing (distressed securities and merger arbitrage), market neutral strategies (long/short investing, convertible hedging), global or macro approaches (i.e., complete investing latitude with leverage), and fund of funds structures (i.e., portfolios of hedge funds).

concerned with asset growth, inflation protection, or investment risk empha-sizes asset-only analysis.

The third consideration is the asset-liability analysis, in which assumptions regarding both asset and liability returns are combined in a surplus optimization or cash flow analysis to arrive at a portfolio structure. A plan sponsor worried about duration mismatch or contribution volatility emphasizes this analysis. Unlike the relatively generic asset-only analysis, an asset-liability analysis is, by definition, plan specific and thus defies generalization. For example, defined-benefit plans differ in several structural and philosophical ways:[2]

- *Funded status.* Companies respond differently to their funded status. Some underfunded plans are aggressive in an effort to close the deficit, whereas others are risk averse, fearing the possibility of even larger future contributions. Some overfunded plans are aggressive because of their ability to weather a period of poor investment performance, but others are risk averse because of a desire to preserve the fund surplus.
- *Plan participant characteristics.* The mix of active and retiree liabilities (i.e., plan maturity) and the expected growth rate in these two groups differ from one company to the next, which is reflected in different liability durations. The mix of U.S. and non-U.S. participants also varies among firms.
- *Retirement benefit structure.* The degree to which benefits are protected against inflation differs among firms.
- *Credit rating.* The borrowing cost of the company determines the rate at which liabilities are discounted.
- *Sensitivity to contribution volatility.* Although pension officers generally dislike boosting contributions, the aversion to that possibility in a given year varies among firms. For example, a defined-benefit plan with significant cash flow requirements relative to aggregate firm cash flow probably is very sensitive to contribution volatility and, therefore, is relatively risk intolerant.
- *Asset-liability analysis methodology.* Views differ on whether the accumulated, projected, or indexed benefit obligation (or some other liability metric) is the appropriate basis for surplus optimization. Views also differ on whether surplus optimization or cash flow/contribution analysis is the appropriate approach.

When combined with assumptions regarding asset performance, the specific philosophies and structural characteristics of a pension plan produce a unique optimal asset mix that *may* differ considerably from the results of the

---

[2]Peskin (1997) provides an excellent discussion of the important issues facing a defined-benefit plan.

asset-only analysis.

In practice, most plan sponsors use the consensus portfolio as a starting point and then make modest adjustments to that portfolio based on the relative importance assigned to the results of the asset-only and asset-liability analyses. When all three influences—consensus peer portfolio, asset-only analysis, and asset-liability analysis—point to a similar portfolio structure, the plan sponsor is in the enviable position of having all bases covered. When the three asset allocations differ significantly, however, the plan sponsor must make some difficult trade-offs among interest rate sensitivity, asset growth, contribution volatility, and peer positioning.[3]

Many plan sponsors have demonstrated through their policy portfolios that rather than risk an atypical asset allocation significantly underperforming that of their peers in a given year, they prefer to deal with the consequences of an asset-liability mismatch, wagering that patience with the stock market will overcome the effects of interest rate cycles. During the 1993–97 period, this preference had a fairly benign effect. Based on the Salomon Smith Barney Pension Liability Index, liability growth in a typical U.S. plan in 1993 and 1995 exceeded asset returns by an average of 11 percent a year. In 1994 and 1996, the opposite occurred, with asset returns outpacing liability returns by 12 percent a year. In 1997, assets and liabilities grew by roughly the same amount. Therefore, despite one of the greatest stock market rallies in U.S. history, the surplus in many pension funds did not improve dramatically over this five-year period.

Obviously, each plan must be mindful of its liability structure. Given the idiosyncrasies of asset-liability analysis, the recommendations in this monograph reflect only the consensus and asset-only considerations. However, setting aside liability considerations does not undermine the general conclusions reached in this monograph. Although heavy reliance on asset-liability analysis *may* justify lower international equity targets than those presented in Chapter 2, many plan sponsors weight the three considerations more equally.[4]

Liability considerations, therefore, cannot be used selectively to justify a

---

[3]Several authors have proposed approaches that incorporate both asset-only and asset-liability considerations. Two examples are Sharpe and Tint (1990) and Leibowitz, Kogelman, and Bader (1992).

[4]Partially hedged international equity offers approximately half the correlation with U.S. liabilities provided by U.S. equity. An asset liability analysis will penalize international equity for this characteristic. However, an asset-liability framework does not eliminate the uncertainty surrounding the expected performance difference between U.S. and international equity. Therefore, one must be careful about making casual return assumptions and implicitly placing disproportionate emphasis upon the relatively low elasticity of international stock returns to changes in U.S. interest rates.

©The Research Foundation of the ICFA

low international equity exposure—particularly when the policy portfolio reflects far more consequential inconsistencies with the asset-liability analysis than the global equity mix. Such inconsistencies fall into three categories:

- *Bond portfolio structure.* Most plan sponsors measure their U.S. bond managers against the Lehman Brothers Aggregate Bond Index. The 4–5 year duration of this popular index is far shorter than the 10–12-year duration of most pension plan liabilities.
- *Stock–bond mix.* Given the relatively low duration of the bond portfolio, the typical 60 percent allocation to equity often appears excessive in an asset-liability framework.
- *Inflation hedge structure.* U.S. stocks are often classified as an inflation hedge, yet investments such as inflation-indexed bonds and, to a lesser extent, real estate and commodities provide more-direct inflation protection.[5] The magnitude of its expected return, not its inflation-hedging properties per se, allows U.S. equity to fill this role. Ironically, this conclusion also applies to international equity, but the possibility that it will outperform U.S. equity is often de-emphasized in favor of highlighting its liability hedging deficiencies.

---

[5]Inflation-linked bonds are not a panacea, because pension liabilities are tied more closely to compensation growth than to the retail price inflation that such bonds hedge. Since its inception, the U.S. Employment Cost Index for private compensation has outpaced the U.S. Consumer Price Index cumulatively by 18 percent. Over that time, the correlation between the two inflation indexes was 0.65. Inflation-indexed bonds thus introduce inflation basis risk.

References

Adler, Michael, and Bhaskar Prasad. 1992. "On Universal Currency Hedges." *Journal of Financial and Quantitative Analysis* (March):19–38.

Adler, Michael, and David Simon. 1986. "Exchange Risk Surprises in International Portfolios." *Journal of Portfolio Management* (Winter):44–53.

Adler, Michael, and Bruno Solnik. 1990. "The Individuality of 'Universal' Hedging." *Financial Analysts Journal* (May/June):7–8.

Akdogan, Haluk. 1996. "A Suggested Approach to Country Selection in International Portfolio Diversification." *Journal of Portfolio Management* (Fall):33–39.

Allen, D.E., and G. MacDonald. 1995. "The Long-Run Gains from International Equity Diversification: Australian Evidence from Cointegration Tests." *Applied Financial Economics,* vol. 5, no. 1:33–42.

Barry, Christopher B., John W. Peavy III, and Mauricio Rodriguez. 1997. *Emerging Stock Markets: Risk, Return, and Performance*. Charlottesville, VA: Research Foundation of the ICFA.

Beckers, Stan, Gregory Connor, and Ross Curds. 1996. "National Versus Global Influences on Equity Returns." *Financial Analysts Journal* (March/April):31–39.

Bekaert, Geert, Claude B. Erb, Campbell R. Harvey, and Tadas E. Viskanta. 1997. "What Matters for Emerging Equity Market Investments." *Emerging Markets Quarterly* (Summer):17–46.

Bekaert, Geert, and Campbell R. Harvey. 1995. "Time-Varying World Market Integration." *Journal of Finance* (June):403–44.

Bergstrom, Gary L. 1975. "A New Route to Higher Returns and Lower Risks." *Journal of Portfolio Management* (Fall):30–38.

Black, Fischer. 1989. "Universal Hedging: Optimizing Currency Risk and Reward in International Equity Portfolios." *Financial Analysts Journal* (July/August):16–22.

Braccia, Joseph A. 1995. "An Analysis of Currency Overlays for U.S. Pension Plans." *Journal of Portfolio Management* (Fall):88–93.

Brinson, Gary P., L. Randolph Hood, and Gilbert L. Beebower. 1986. "Determinants of Portfolio Performance." *Financial Analysts Journal* (July/August):39–44.

Brinson, Gary P., Brian D. Singer, and Gilbert L. Beebower. 1991. "Determinants of Portfolio Performance II." *Financial Analysts Journal* (May/June):40–48.

Browne, Remi J. 1987. "The Case for Not Hedging." *Benefits & Compensation International* (November):7–10.

Chopra, Vijay K., and William T. Ziemba. 1993. "The Effects of Errors in Means, Variances, and Covariances on Optimal Portfolio Choice." *Journal of Portfolio Management* (Winter):6–12.

Dencik, Peter J. 1997. "International Equity Diversification for Pension Funds: A Comment." *Journal of Investing* (Spring):32–33.

Divecha, Arjun B., Jaime Drach, and Dan Stefek. 1992. "Emerging Markets: A Quantitative Perspective." *Journal of Portfolio Management* (Fall):41–50.

Eaker, Mark, and Dwight Grant. 1990. "Currency Hedging Strategies for Internationally Diversified Equity Portfolios." *Journal of Portfolio Management* (Fall):30–32.

Eaker, Mark R., Dwight M. Grant, and Nelson Woodard. 1991. "International Diversification and Hedging: A Japanese and U.S. Perspective." *Journal of Economics and Business* (November):363–74.

Erb, Claude B., Campbell R. Harvey, and Tadas E. Viskanta. 1994. "Forecasting International Equity Correlations." *Financial Analysts Journal* (November/December):32–45.

———. 1997. "The Making of an Emerging Market." *Emerging Markets Quarterly* (Spring):14–19.

Errunza, Vihang R. 1997. "Research on Emerging Markets: Past, Present, and Future." *Emerging Markets Quarterly* (Fall):5–18.

Espitia, M., and R. Santamaria. 1994. "International Diversification among the Capital Markets of the EEC." *Applied Financial Economics*, vol. 4, no. 1:1–10.

Ezra, D. Don. 1991. "Asset Allocation by Surplus Optimization." *Financial Analysts Journal* (January/February):51–57.

Fouse, William L. 1992. "Allocating Assets across Country Markets." *Journal of Portfolio Management* (Winter):20–27.

French, Kenneth R., and James M. Poterba. 1991. "Investor Diversification and International Equity Markets." *AEA Papers and Proceedings on Behavioral Finance* (May):222–26.

Froot, Kenneth A. 1993. "Currency Hedging over Long Horizons." Working Paper No. 4355. National Bureau of Economic Research.

Gastineau, Gary L. 1995. "The Currency Hedging Decision: A Search for Synthesis in Asset Allocation." *Financial Analysts Journal* (May/June):8–17.

Grauer, Frederick L.A., Robert H. Litzenberger, and Richard E. Stehle. 1976. "Sharing Rules and Equilibrium in an International Capital Market under Uncertainty." *Journal of Financial Economics*, vol. 3, no. 3:233–56.

Griffin, John M., and G. Andrew Karolyi. 1995. "Another Look at the Role of the Industrial Structure of Markets for International Diversification Strategies." Working Paper. (October).

Griffin, Mark W. 1997. "Why Do Pension and Insurance Portfolios Hold So Few International Assets?" *Journal of Portfolio Management* (Summer):45–50.

Grinold, Richard, Andrew Rudd, and Dan Stefek. 1989. "Global Factors: Fact or Fiction?" *Journal of Portfolio Management* (Fall):79–88.

Grubel, H.G. 1968. "Internationally Diversified Portfolios: Welfare Gains and Capital Flows." *American Economic Review* (December):1299–1314.

Halpern, Philip. 1993. "Investing Abroad: A Review of Capital Market Integration and Manager Performance." *Journal of Portfolio Management* (Winter):47–57.

Hammond, Dennis R. 1996. "Equity Diversification Internationally." *Journal of Investing* (Summer):36–42.

Heston, Steven L., and K. Geert Rouwenhorst. 1995. "Industry and Country Effects in International Stock Returns." *Journal of Portfolio Management* (Spring):53–58.

Hunter, John E., and Daniel R. Coggin. 1990. "An Analysis of the Diversification Benefit from International Equity Investment." *Journal of Portfolio Management* (Fall):33–36.

Jacquillat, Bertrand, and Bruno Solnik. 1978. "Multinationals Are Poor Tools for Diversification." *Journal of Portfolio Management* (Winter):8–12.

Jahnke, William. 1997. "The Asset Allocation Hoax." *Journal of Financial Planning* (February):109–113.

Johnson, Larry J., and Carl H. Walther. 1991–92. "The Value of International Equity Diversification: An Empirical Test." *Journal of Applied Business Research*, vol. 8, no. 1:38–44.

Jorion, Philippe. 1985. "International Portfolio Diversification with Estimation Risk." *Journal of Business*, vol. 58, no. 3:259–78.

————. 1989. "Asset Allocation with Hedged and Unhedged Foreign Stocks and Bonds." *Journal of Portfolio Management* (Summer):49–54.

————. 1994. "Mean–Variance Analysis of Currency Overlays." *Financial Analysts Journal* (May/June):48–56.

Jorion, Philippe, and Leonid Roisenberg. 1993. "Synthetic International Diversification." *Journal of Portfolio Management* (Winter):65–74.

Keppler, Michael, and Heydon D. Traub. 1993. "The Small-Country Effect: Small Markets Beat Large Markets." *Journal of Investing* (Fall):17–24.

Khoury, Nabil, Jean-Marc Martel, and Pierre Yourougou. 1994. "A Multicriterion Approach to Country Selection for Global Index Funds." *Global Finance Journal*, vol. 5, no. 1:17–35.

King, Mervyn, Enrique Sentana, and Sushil Wadhwani. 1994. "Volatility and Links between National Stock Markets." *Econometrica* (July):901–33.

Kritzman, Mark P., and Katrina F. Sherrerd, eds. 1989. *Managing Currency Risk*. Charlottesville, VA: Institute of Chartered Financial Analysts.

Landes, William, and Stephen Gorman. 1997. "Pitfalls in Strategic Asset Allocation." *Journal of Pension Plan Investing* (Winter):94–106.

Lee, Adrian F. 1987. "International Asset and Currency Allocation." *Journal of Portfolio Management* (Fall):68–73.

Leibowitz, Martin L. 1986. "Total Portfolio Duration: A New Perspective on Asset Allocation." *Financial Analysts Journal* (September/October):18–29.

————. 1994. "Funding Ratio Return." *Journal of Portfolio Management* (Fall):39–47.

Leibowitz, Martin L., and Roy D. Henriksson. 1988. "Portfolio Optimization within a Surplus Framework." *Financial Analysts Journal* (March/April):43–51.

Leibowitz, Martin L., Stanley Kogelman, and Lawrence N. Bader. 1992. "Asset Performance and Surplus Control: A Dual-Shortfall Approach." *Journal of Portfolio Management* (Winter):28–37.

©The Research Foundation of the ICFA

Lessard, Donald R. 1976. "World, Country, and Industry Relationships in Equity Returns: Implications for Risk Reduction through International Diversification." *Financial Analysts Journal* (January/February):32–38.

Levy, Haim, and Marshall Sarnat. 1970. "International Diversification of Investment Portfolios." *American Economic Review* (September):668–75.

————. 1978. "Exchange Rate Risk and the Optimal Diversification of Foreign Currency Holdings." *Journal of Money, Credit, and Banking* (November):453–63.

Lin, Wen-Ling, Robert F. Engle, and Takatoshi Ito. 1994. "Do Bulls and Bears Move across Borders? International Transmission of Stock Returns and Volatility." *Review of Financial Studies* (Fall):507–38.

Longin, François, and Bruno Solnik. 1995. "Is the Correlation in International Equity Returns Constant: 1960–90?" *Journal of International Money and Finance*, vol. 14, no. 1:3–26.

MacBeth, James D., David C. Emanuel, and Craig E. Heatter. 1994. "An Investment Strategy for Defined Benefit Plans." *Financial Analysts Journal* (May/June):34–41.

Madura, Jeff, and Wallace Reiff. 1985. "A Hedge Strategy for International Portfolios." *Journal of Portfolio Management* (Fall):70–74.

Markowitz, Harry S. 1959. *Portfolio Selection: Efficient Diversification of Investments*. New York: John Wiley & Sons.

————. 1991. *Portfolio Selection*. Cambridge, MA: Basil Blackwell.

Meese, Richard. 1990. "Currency Fluctuations in the Post-Bretton Woods Era." *Journal of Economic Perspectives* (Winter):117–34.

Michaud, Richard O., Gary L. Bergstrom, Ronald D. Frashure, and Brian K. Wolahan. 1996. "Twenty Years of International Equity Investing." *Journal of Portfolio Management* (Fall):9–22.

Odier, Patrick, and Bruno Solnik. 1993. "Lessons for International Asset Allocation." *Financial Analysts Journal* (March/April):60–74.

Peavy, John W. III, ed. 1994. *Managing Emerging Market Portfolios*. Charlottesville, VA: AIMR.

Perold, André F., and Evan C. Schulman. 1988. "The Free Lunch in Currency Hedging: Implications for Investment Policy and Performance Standards." *Financial Analysts Journal* (May/June):45–50.

Peskin, K. Stuart. 1997. "Emerging Markets Benchmarks: Understanding an Evolving Asset Class." *Emerging Markets Quarterly* (Spring):27–32.

Peskin, Michael W. 1997. "Asset Allocation and Funding Policy for Corporate-Sponsored Defined-Benefit Pension Plans." *Journal of Portfolio Management* (Winter):66–73.

Peterson, Craig A. 1996. "Risk and Return Characteristics of American Depositary Receipts." *Journal of Investing* (Fall):74–85.

Rogoff, Kenneth. 1996. "The Purchasing Power Parity Puzzle." *Journal of Economic Literature* (June):647–68.

Roll, Richard. 1992. "Industrial Structure and the Comparative Behavior of International Stock Market Indices." *Journal of Finance* (March):3–41.

Senchack, Andrew J., and William L. Beedles. 1980. "Is Indirect International Diversification Desirable?" *Journal of Portfolio Management* (Winter):49–57.

Sharpe, William F., and Lawrence G. Tint. 1990. "Liabilities—A New Approach." *Journal of Portfolio Management* (Winter):5–10.

Siegel, Jeremy J. 1994. *Stocks for the Long Run*. Chicago, IL: Irwin Professional.

Sinquefield, Rex A. 1996. "Where Are the Gains from International Diversification?" *Financial Analysts Journal* (January/February):8–14.

Solnik, Bruno H. 1974a. "An Equilibrium Model of the International Capital Market." *Journal of Economic Theory* (July/August):500–24.

———. 1974b. "Why Not Diversify Internationally Rather Than Domestically?" *Financial Analysts Journal* (July/August):48–54.

———. 1993. "Currency Hedging and Siegel's Paradox: On Black's Universal Hedging Rule." *Review of International Economics*, vol. 1, no. 2:180–87.

———. 1996. *International Investments*, 3rd ed. Reading, MA: Addison-Wesley.

Solnik, Bruno, Cyril Boucrelle, and Yann Le Fur. 1996. "International Market Correlation and Volatility." *Financial Analysts Journal* (September/October):17–34.

Solnik, Bruno, and Bernard Noetzlin. 1982. "Optimal International Asset Allocation." *Journal of Portfolio Management* (Fall):11–21.

Sorenson, Eric H., Joseph J. Mezrich, and Dilip N. Thadani. 1993. "Currency Hedging through Portfolio Optimization." *Journal of Portfolio Management* (Spring):78–85.

Speidell, Lawrence S., and Ross Sappenfield. 1992. "Global Diversification in a Shrinking World." *Journal of Portfolio Management* (Fall):57–67.

Stone, Douglas. 1992. "The Emerging Markets and Strategic Asset Allocation." *Journal of Investing* (Summer):40–45.

Strongin, Steve, Melanie Petsch, and Colin Fenton. 1997. "Global Equity Portfolios and the Business Cycle." Goldman Sachs Global Portfolio Analysis (April).

Stulz, Rene M. 1981. "A Model of International Asset Pricing." *Journal of Financial Economics* (December):383–406.

Sudweeks, Bryan. 1997. "From Extreme to Mainstream: The Strategic Case for Emerging Markets." *Emerging Markets Quarterly* (Winter):39–46.

Thomas, Lee R. 1988. "Currency Risks in International Equity Portfolios." *Financial Analysts Journal* (March/April):68–71.

Tobin, James. 1958. "Liquidity Preference as Behavior towards Risk." *Review of Economic Studies* (February):65–86.

Wilcox, Jarrod W. 1992. "Global Investing in Emerging Markets." *Financial Analysts Journal* (January/February):15–19.

———. 1994. "EAFE is for Wimps." *Journal of Portfolio Management* (Spring):68–75.

———. 1997. "Better Emerging Market Portfolios." *Emerging Markets Quarterly* (Summer):5–16.

Winston, Kenneth J., and Jeffery V. Bailey. 1996. "Investment Policy Implications of Currency Hedging." *Journal of Portfolio Management* (Summer):50–57.

Selected AIMR Publications

AIMR Performance Presentation Standards Handbook, 2nd edition, 1996

Credit Analysis Around the World, 1998

Deregulation of the Electric Utility Industry, 1997

Derivatives in Portfolio Management, 1998

Economic Analysis for Investment Professionals, 1997

Finding Reality in Reported Earnings, 1997

Global Bond Management, 1997

Global Equity Investing, 1996

Global Portfolio Management, 1996

Implementing Global Equity Strategy: Spotlight on Asia, 1997

Investing in Small-Cap and Microcap Securities, 1997

Investing Worldwide VIII: Developments in Global Portfolio Management, 1997

Managing Currency Risk, 1997

Merck & Company: A Comprehensive Equity Valuation Analysis, 1996
Randall S. Billingsley, CFA

Readings in Venture Capital, 1997

Standards of Practice Casebook, 1996

Standards of Practice Handbook, 7th edition, 1996

A full catalog of publications is available on AIMR's World Wide Web site at **www.aimr.org**; or you may write to AIMR, P.O. Box 3668, Charlottesville, VA 22903 U.S.A.; call 1-804-980-3668; fax 1-804-963-6826; or e-mail **info@aimr.org** to receive a free copy. All prices are subject to change.